MAX WEGNER

GREEK
MASTERWORKS
OF ART

TRANSLATED BY CHARLOTTE LA RUE

———————————————

GEORGE BRAZILLER

NEW YORK 1961

TRANSLATED FROM THE GERMAN BY CHARLOTTE LA RUE

LIBRARY OF CONGRESS CATALOG CARD NUMBER: 61–8475

ORIGINALLY PUBLISHED IN GERMAN UNDER THE TITLE OF
'MEISTERWERKE DER GRIECHEN', COPYRIGHT 1955 BY HOLBEIN-VERLAG.
PROTECTED UNDER THE BERNE CONVENTION.

PUBLISHED IN 1961 IN THE ENGLISH LANGUAGE BY ARRANGEMENT
WITH THE AUTHOR, MAX WEGNER.

INQUIRY SHOULD BY MADE TO THE PUBLISHER,
GEORGE BRAZILLER, INC., 215 PARK AVENUE SOUTH, NEW YORK 3, N.Y.

PRINTED IN SWITZERLAND

Table of Contents

CHRONOLOGICAL TABLE

	DATE	HISTORY	BUILDINGS	
	12th Century	Doric migration		
PROTOGEOMETRIC				
GEOMETRIC	756	Cyme founded. Beginning of Greek colonization		
ARCHAIC	688 Middle of 7th Century	Gela founded Rise of the Tyrants		
	594	Solon elected archon with unlimited power	Korkyra, Temple of Artemis	Fig. 131–133
			Athens, Old Temple of Athena I	Fig. 134–136
	566	Establishment of the Panathenaea		
			Paestum, Enneastylos	Fig. 122
			Delphi, Temple of Apollo	Fig. 101
	514	Tyrannicide in Athens	Delphi, Siphnian Treasury	Fig. 137–142
	510	Expulsion of the Tyrants from Athens	Athens, Old Temple of Athena II	Fig. 143
			Delphi, Athenian Treasury	Fig. 117
CLASSIC	480/79	Destruction of the Athenian Acropolis by the Persians		
			Olympia, Temple of Zeus	Fig. 124, 125, 144–153
			Paestum, Temple of Poseidon	Fig. 118, 119
	429	Death of Pericles	Athens, Parthenon	Fig. 126, 127, 157–166
	431–404	Peloponnesian War		
			Athenian Acropolis, Erechtheum	Fig. 99, 121, 129, 130
			Athenian Acropolis, Temple of Nike	Fig. 128
			Delphi, Tholos	Fig. 120
HELLENISTIC	336–323	Alexander the Great		
			Delos, Hellenistic Hall	Fig. 116
	162–150	Demetrius I of Syria		

6

SCULPTURE		CERAMICS		
		Protogeometric vessels	Fig. 34–36	PROTOGEOMETRIC
Tripods	Fig. 43, 44	Geometric vessels	Fig. 37–42, 55	GEOMETRIC
Bronze statuettes	Fig. 45–50, 56	Hydria from Analatos	Fig. 54	
Statuette of a youth from Delphi	Fig. 51, 52			
Nikandre	Fig. 105			
Bronze relief from Olympia	Fig. 57	Small Cretan jug	Fig. 106	
'Woman of Auxerre'	Fig. 107	Protocorinthian Chigi jug	Fig. 66	
Kouros from the Dipylon	Fig. 53	Rhodian jug	Fig. 92	
Kleobis and Biton	Fig. 16			
Hera from Olympia	Fig. 62			
Street of Lions in Delos	Fig. 102	Corinthian crater	Fig. 67	
Naxian sphinx	Fig. 103	Corinthian hydria	Fig. 68	ARCHAIC
Calf-bearer from the Acropolis	Fig. 104	Klitias and Ergotimos	Fig. 71, 72	
Nike from Delos	Fig. 7	Exekias; Amasis	Fig. 74, 75, 77; 73	
Kouroi from Tenea and Melos	Fig. 14, 15, 17	Andokides; Epiktetos	Fig. 90, 91; 78	
Korai from the Acropolis	Fig. 108–111	Euphronios	Fig. 81, 86, 88, 89	
Stele of Aristion	Fig. 13	Euthymides; Sosias	Fig. 87; 79	
Kouros statuette from the Acropolis	Fig. 19, 20	Panaitios Painter	Fig. 85	
Apollo from Piombino	Fig. 1, 18	Brygos Painter	Fig. 93, 94	
Youth by Critios	Fig. 23	Antiphon Painter	Fig. 21	
Charioteer from Delphi	Fig. 28, 29	Douris	Fig. 24, 80	
Torso of a youth, Florence	Fig. 25	Pistoxenos	Fig. 95, 96	
'Blond Head' from the Acropolis	Fig. 26	Penthesilea Painter	Fig. 82–84	
Throne of Ludovisi	Fig. 154			
Stele Giustiniani	Fig. 12			
Poseidon from Cape Artemision	Fig. 27			
Phidias and Polykletos		Kleophon Painter	Fig. 98	CLASSIC
Youth, Paris	Fig. 31	Orpheus Painter	Fig. 97	
Youth, Athens	Fig. 30	Oinochoe	Fig. 63, 64	
Stele from Salamis	Fig. 11			
Dying child of Niobe	Fig. 155, 156			
Nike of Paionios	Fig. 6			
Stele of Hegeso	Fig. 10			
Stele of Ameinokleia	Fig. 9			
Stele from the Ilissos	Fig. 8			
Lysippos				
Resting Satyr	Fig. 4			
Nike from Samothrace	Fig. 5			HELLENISTIC
Ruler	Fig. 3			
Venus of Milo	Fig. 2			

Opposite the title page: Figure 1. Head of the Apollo from Piombino. Detail of Fig. 18.

THE VENUS OF MILO, the Aphrodite who was discovered by chance on the island of Melos   Fig. 2
in 1820, has during the last hundred years become the best known, most beloved, and most
admired of Greek works of art. As Helen was abducted by Paris, she too was taken from her
homeland in romantic fashion although this noteworthy event led to a civil law suit rather
than a Trojan war. Now visitors to the Louvre in Paris are drawn to her irresistibly, by day
and night; and even the most talkative tourist becomes silent, gripped with emotion at the
sight of her as were the old men of Troy, when Helen approached: 'Small blame is it that
Trojans and well-greaved Achaians should for such a woman long time suffer hardships.'
The indescribable and compelling beauty thus expressed by the poet has assumed visible
form in the Venus of Milo. She is fashioned with great perfection to reveal a wholly sensuous beauty, based on an exact study of the natural nude female body. The drapery, which
has slipped down to the hips in magnificently intricate folds, and flutters restlessly in light
and shadow, heightens the contrasting impression of silken smoothness given by the nude
surfaces of the figure above. The slender body grows upward from the robe, slightly turned
and curved; and its fresh mobility is consummated in the tilting of the elegant head. Her
soft gaze is lost in the infinite. The artist has so completely captured the basic nature of the
goddess of beauty and love, the power through which she acts and affects others, that she
seems to embody beauty itself in 'noble simplicity and quiet magnitude.' Such an image of
beauty in the universal sense is the embodiment and perfection of fine art at its greatest:
thus the Venus of Milo fittingly represents the classical ideal of beauty. However, not only
the ideal, but classicism itself has its history and its destiny.

'Much admired and abused,' like Helen, Greek antiquity confronts us – us, its descendants
and discoverers. We inscribe 'Hellas' on our banners; the accomplishments of the Greeks
challenge us to change our own lives; or we attack antiquity in the name of modernity. It is
not within the intent of this book to join the argument, although the validity and applica-
bility of the classical ideal are today called into question.

'Classic' was first used to designate a perfect standard in ancient Rome, when the exem-
plary Greek poets of the fifth century B.C. were called classics. Later the concept of the
classic was enlarged to include the entire historical epoch of Greek and Roman antiquity.
Finally, in the evolution of ideas, the word was elevated to a general concept for any time
of flowering. Critics spoke, for example, of 'classic baroque,' meaning the high baroque of

the seventeenth century, completely opposed to the antique in many of its forms of expression. On the other hand, they labeled later phases of antiquity, particularly Hellenism, the 'baroque of classical antiquity.' A dictum of Benedetto Croce shows how greatly the meaning of this word has changed and expanded: 'Art is by definition always classical, and romantic art was also classical, as soon as it was really classic.' Here again 'classic' serves as an evaluation, by no means limited to antiquity, but rather a designation for anything which is perfectly executed. It must now be demonstrated in each individual case in what sense a work or an epoch of antiquity can be called classic.

But does beauty of pure form and line, beauty that is pleasing to the eye, as we meet it in the Venus of Milo, remain the proof of perfection in art, as modern aesthetic theories (particularly those dealing with classicism and idealism) sometimes claim? Is such an ideal beauty a general characteristic of the human images of antiquity, as is commonly believed, and as classic sculpture would lead us to expect? Winckelmann, the first man to write a 'History of the Art of Antiquity,' held firm to his aesthetic theory that beauty is the highest aim of art; but, in his observations and explanations, he also admitted the validity of other forms of expression among the Greeks. With them, beauty is something taken for granted, rather than an aesthetic postulate.

That highest beauty which 'is in God' certainly does not account for the masterly effect of the splendid bronze statue of a bold and powerful male nude, created about half a century earlier than the Venus of Milo; it impresses much more

Fig. 3

2   *Aphrodite of Melos (Venus of Milo).*
    Marble. 204 cm. high.

10

through the characteristic, through its particular stamp. Unbalanced, with the axis of his body variously disarranged, needing the support of the lance in his left hand, the exuberantly powerful youth stands in reality, in his own definite area of motion, where he struts, reaches out or repulses with his arms, shifts his legs, arches his chest; and his gaze seeks a definite goal. The head has so much character that the conjecture has been made that the statue is a portrait of an Hellenic ruler, Demetrius 1 of Syria, in his youth. Although this figure of a youth appears to us a definite personality, he is not a unique individual in our modern sense. This may account for the recent suggestion that the statue has a mythological significance and may represent one of the two Dioscuri. This indefiniteness is typical of the Greek work of art. Rulers and heroes, and even youthful gods whose outstanding characteristic was physical proficiency, were portrayed in the same manner, as strong, healthy, well-developed nude youths: in this case, an excessively muscular, athletic type. Alexander the Great, the first Hellenic ruler in history, claimed to excel Herakles in strength, and had himself portrayed in this manner. The characteristic aims, not at the individual, but at the type; yet these same Hellenistic artists were destined to lay the groundwork for a development of portraiture to extremes of exact representation, hiding not even the deformed and the ugly.

The Aphrodite of Melos, thanks to her divine, ideal beauty, and the so-called ruler, thanks to his realistic character, can be experienced directly and immediately by the modern observer. A

Fig. 4 third work may further elucidate this self-evi-

3 Hellenistic Ruler. Bronze. 222 cm. high.

dent nature of Greek sculpture: the resting satyr, which originated a century earlier, at the height of the Hellenistic period. A crude son of nature, a carefree savage, has thrown himself down on a mountain slope, on the skin of an animal, and stretches out in sleep, a sleep so natural that you can almost perceive the quiet breath passing in and out of his lightly parted lips. The figure is completely open to the air and light; his limbs sprawl in various directions; the powerful modeling of the head, the torso and the legs, and the expression of the features become most effective in a strong contrast of light and shadow. In the presence of such a statue, it is quite understandable that we are almost forced to conceive of a Hellenistic baroque. Actually the striking similarity, cutting across time, to the modern baroque can be demonstrated in this case. Lorenzo Bernini became acquainted with this Greek original immediately after it had been discovered at the Castle of St. Angelo in Rome. He restored the lacking portions of the statue with stucco, particularly the whole right leg and the left forearm; and toward the end of his activity as a sculptor, he created something quite similar in his Allegory of Truth. But in Bernini's Allegory of Truth, the thought he intended to express completely overweighed the sensuous aspects, while in the Satyr the essential meaning is fully expressed in the form of the statue itself, 'an image of self-possessed, simple nature' (Winckelmann). The characteristics typical of a satyr, the horse tail and pointed ears, are treated inconspicuously; the panther skin seems to serve quite naturally for the purpose of comfort. The observer does not have to know anything about the mythology of satyrs; the meaning is plainly evident from the representation. If we accept Hegel's definition of the classic as 'that which is meaningful in itself, and means itself,' we find it here. Just as the Aphrodite is the very shape of divine beauty itself, so this demon of the wilderness is the embodiment of the divine that resides in the primitive world of nature, even in sleep itself, in that mysterious mid-day hush of the hot south which is known as the sleep of Pan.

Fig. 5 Another somewhat more recent statue from the height of the Hellenistic period, the Winged Victory of Samothrace, cannot be understood so immediately to its full extent by the modern observer. It needs some additional explanation. A mighty female figure with giant wings appears to have just set foot on the prow of a ship, after the powerful motion of descending flight, and seeks support against the storm. The headwinds press her garment against her body and swirl its wide folds like waves on a rocky coast. The figure's spontaneous motion and the violent pressure from outside act together to increase the effectiveness and rich variety of this statue. In contrast to a static, self-encompassed shape, this agitated figure is open to all the dimensions; her configuration implies what is around her, wind, air and sea. It has been supposed that the lost arms might have held a trumpet, but a recently discovered hand leads us to guess that she may have held out a victor's fillet. The figure represents Nike, the wind-swift goddess of victory, sent forth by Zeus to achieve a naval victory (indicated by the prow of the ship on which she stands). It is a triumphal monument, probably celebrating the victory of Rhodes over Antiochos III in 190 B.C. This historical fact is a welcome help in dating the statue. Usually in determining the periods of Greek works of art we must depend primarily upon evolutionary considerations.

12

4   Resting Satyr. Marble. 215 cm. high.   *5   Nike from Samothrace. Marble. 200 cm. high.*

Monuments in commemoration of a victory have always been customary in ancient oriental cultures, and there were a number of them in Greek antiquity, particularly ones of this kind, in the image of a god. The idea that all success, every fortunate achievement, whether in war or in the friendly rivalries of physical and poetic contests, is a gift of the gods was always present among the Greeks. From the sanctuary of Olympia there has been Fig. 6 preserved for us a triumphal monument by a sculptor whose name is known, the Nike of Paionios. The allied Messenians and Naupaktonians consecrated her to commemorate their victory over the Spartans about 421 B.C., two and a quarter centuries before the Victory of Samothrace. An entirely different concept and different idea of form dominated the sculptor. The Nike of Samothrace has her place on the victorious ship, seems to stand in the midst of the busy world, and, as originally erected, was seen from a definite point of view by the observer. On the other hand, the Nike of Paionios was raised high on a slender three-sided pillar and placed in the sanctuary of Olympia, near the Temple of Father Zeus. With raised wings (which have been lost, for the most part) she appears to float along; an eagle, gliding directly beneath her feet, shows clearly that she is hovering in the air. In the statue's original condition, a broad mantle swells out like a sail behind the Nike's delicate body, against which the wind presses her robe, so that its shape is very distinct, and contrasted in its supple plasticity to the irregular froth of folds at the sides. In the Nike of Samothrace, an emotional use of sculptural means aims at a magnificent artistic effect; while, in

13

6 *Nike by Paionios. Marble. 216 cm. high.*   7 *Nike from Delos. Marble. 90 cm. high.*

the Nike of Paionios, all form is skilfully used for the purpose of rendering tangible the divine actor, the swift messenger from the heights of Olympus. Instead of the stormy movements of violent action, the solemn calm of a divine presence holds sway. If the Nike of Paionios seems still to belong to the 'blessed' gods, 'living untroubled,' in the words of Homer, then the Nike of Samothrace is divine power and action itself; her form embodies a god-sent, extraordinary event.

Fig. 7   A third Nike, a much more ancient statue from the period shortly before the middle of the sixth century, which was found on the sacred island of Delos, is infinitely far removed from what we think of as tangible reality. We must fill out the fragmentary condition of this statue by imagining two large crescent-shaped wings spread symmetrically behind her shoulders, sharply angled arms and legs, and a robe hanging below the legs to show the figure is floating. Probably the Nike of Delos was not set up on a pillar alone, but instead was installed as the crowning figure on the roof of a temple. The ancient symbolism of the knee bent in running indicates that she is hastening along, and her head is turned directly

14

toward the person who approaches her. In comparison to the Nike of Paionios, here divinity is not incorporated in a form that is easily comprehended; instead, she is a wholly divine being, with her own reality. This ancient statue, with its unaccustomed bearing of trunk and legs and its angularity, may strike us as archaic. In our judgment the artistic virtuosity of the Victory of Samothrace may be more pleasing. But this is not a fitting criterion. It is a subjective, aesthetic judgment, not a real, objective one. We think we discern, however difficult this is to express, that in the one case it was a matter of an absolute goddess becoming an image, and in the other case, a matter of the artistic realization of a divine apparition.

In our observation of Greek masterpieces and our attempt to understand them correctly, we will at times have to balance meaning and art against each other. At the beginning we observed several Hellenistic statues, judging them, as is our habit, as works of art. In this process, they revealed a great deal to us because in the Hellenistic epoch apparently individual artistic accomplishment carried a great deal of weight. But as far as Greek statues are concerned, it is by no means self-evident that we should start with appreciation of artistic achievement, as we do with modern works of art. The three Victories that have just been compared are individual representatives of three corresponding epochs in Greek plastic art, the archaic, the classical, and the Hellenistic, each statue being a work from its time of flowering, the 'classic' period of that particular epoch. Not only were the differences of artistic form great; more important, the meaning, significance, and content differed radically in the three statues. For each epoch it is necessary to find out about its own characteristics, and to measure its achievements in their light. If statues are to gain their validity at one time from outside, from an objective viewpoint, and at another time from within, as subjectively apprehended, then we cannot count on continuing standards of an aesthetic sort; they leave us in the lurch. We will therefore have to be cautious about using customary ideas, and will rather seek to extract its essence from each object itself.

Is it not then, a vain undertaking, conditioned by our over-emphasis on history, to want to possess the Greek masterworks more fully, beyond what they themselves disclose to our spontaneous capacity to experience, our emotions, and our taste? During the last few centuries, pleasure and understanding have gone hand in hand, and have gradually – aided amazingly by the good luck of enterprising excavators – gained dominion over the whole of Greek and Roman antiquity to its entire extent of a millennium and a half. Dedication to the antique and enthusiasm for it were the trailblazers of archeological research. The artists of the early Renaissance, to further their own artistic endeavors, studied the Roman remains which stood right before their eyes – buildings, historical reliefs, and sarcophagi. Michelangelo lauded the Laocoön as a miracle of art, and received creative stimulation from it. Bernini's receptiveness to the satyr from the height of the Hellenistic period has already been mentioned. Winckelmann, who grew up in the late baroque period and was a founder of classicism in the middle of the eighteenth century, admired the Laocoön group, the torso in Belvedere and the Apollo there, works of late Hellenism and of the 'fine style' of the fourth century B.C. Goethe, following Winckelmann, began with the same preferences until, in old age, he saw in the sublime classical sculptures of the Parthenon the utmost achievement of human artistic striving, for the sake of which, if need be, he would do without everything else. The severe classical sculptures in the Temple of Zeus in Olympia won the highest praise, not immediately upon their discovery in the years 1875–1881, but soon thereafter. And, finally, present taste is primarily attuned to the archaic and the very early works. It would even appear that the most modern abstract art and the earliest geometrical forms of Greek expression not only are allied outwardly in their freedom, whether intentional or unconscious, from the natural pattern, but also reveal an even deeper affinity – which poses one of the problems of art itself as it has developed to date. Thus, the question we have just raised, as to the adequacy of past concepts of art when viewing the total sequence of Greek sculpture, is itself a phenomenon of the times. Apparently every epoch, in more or less limited fashion, has its own antiquity and, by and large, appreciation and understanding of the works of the ancients moves against the historical current. This is caused to a great extent by a deep-lying accord of interests and sensibilities. But then this instinctive liking for the work of a particular period gives rise to a desire to evaluate the admired object correctly and to understand it. From what is close at hand and easy to grasp, the art lover presses on to what is older and strange, at first, gradually feels at home with it too, and thus climbs upward, step by step, to the earliest times. Our present project of winning Greek antiquity for a friend may benefit from this observation. We can here attempt nothing further than to show a number of the masterpieces of the Greeks and contribute to a deeper understanding of them. Limitations of space mean that the text must remain fragmentary with respect to the history of Greek art. (The chronological table on pages 6–7 is meant to serve as an over-all view of the sequence of historical epochs in Greek art and of the works mentioned.)

Although consciously foregoing historical justice and symmetry, we will not stop with Hellenism, if we seek to experience the unique Greek contribution to the enrichment of our own lives. Gustav Droysen has defended his glorification of Hellenism with the phrase that it was 'the modern time of antiquity.' We do not want to be guilty of historical injustice, but will calmly confess that Hellenism touches us less, as soon as we no longer deceive ourselves with aesthetic pleasure. The progressive culture of Hellenism was related in many ways to the modern period – of yesterday – and for that reason is directly accessible to us. Above all, it was the time of palaces and city-states, of portrait statues and genre figures, of mural painting and domestic arts, of handicrafts and decoration. All of this is too much a part of our own art world, well known, and has little to say to us, or at most lulls us with a sweet song about how gloriously far we have progressed. On the contrary, we want to weigh anchor for the journey *au fond de l'inconnu pour trouver du nouveau*!' (Baudelaire: 'to the end of the unknown, to find the new!')

In the poem by Baudelaire, just cited, Death is the old helmsman who lifts the anchor. Funeral monuments and the cult of the dead were one of the most important realms in which the Greeks exercised their artistic abilities. Serious thoughts are expressed in these works, and we may gain from them much enlightenment about the ancients' conception of life. At the beginning we place two Attic gravestones from the fourth century B.C., toward the end of which the established classic style was giving way to Hellenism. The earlier of the two, the grave relief of Ameinokleia, reproduces a scene from life in the women's Fig. 9 chambers, and exudes the gentle melancholy of parting. Two servants are waiting upon their mistress; the monument is meant for her, but she is not yet thought of as dead. One servant holds a jewel case, from which she is about to take something. The other kneels before her mistress, busied with putting on her sandal. Ameinokleia touches the top of the kneeling girl's head with a light, tender gesture. The two standing women are not upright, supporting their own weight; instead, they lean against the framing pillars of the small structure, as though their existence lacked proper vitality. All the women in this grave relief are marked with melancholy and the quiet sorrow of coming death. It has been asked, with justice, whether the woman is not being adorned for her final journey.[1] Over this picture, which seems to be taken from life, there lies an ambiguity determined by death. It is a memorial that holds both life and death at once, joins them together beyond the grave, anticipates sorrow for the dead woman in a scene from her life. Nothing strange intrudes' no angel of death, no alien mourning. This work is a participant in death and sorrow, and in that rests its compelling symbolism as a grave monument.

Of another sort is the gravestone from the Ilissos, which originated toward the end of Fig. 8 the late classic period, not long before a law banning luxury, proclaimed by Demetrius of Phaleron in the year 316 B.C., brought an end to large Attic grave sculpture. A naked youth, leaning backward, and an old man, wrapped closely in a mantle and leaning on his staff, both almost life size, face each other, and at their feet is a little boy sitting asleep and a sniffing dog. The handsome youth, whose troubled gaze is lost in the distance, is the deceased. The pillar at the top of two steps, on which he is half sitting, can only be the gravestone, reduced in an unusual manner to serve the artistic purpose of providing a meaningful support for the resting youth. The sorrowing old father gazes, deeply distressed, at his son in the bloom of his youth, close enough for him to touch, but still snatched away by an early death. The boy, who served the deceased, has lost his duties with his lord, is overcome with

8 *Grave stele from the Ilissos. Marble. 168 cm. high.*   9 *Grave stele of Ameinokleia. Marble. 135 cm. high.*

weariness, and symbolizes the nearness of sleep and death. The dog, the youth's faithful companion, sniffs at the foot of the bereaved old man, and forms the only living link between son and father. This completes a mysterious circle of relationships and emotions about the parting that death has decreed. The picture has a remarkable dichotomy. The deceased appears in the most flourishing physical state in contrast to the living man, who seems rather to be the one who has departed, who has been set free. But again the sensuous beauty of the youth's body is questionable because it is empty, without tension. The body holds only beauty and dissolution, while the soul, lonely, wanders far from life in the troubled gaze. No longer certain of that which endures, the youth is now more strongly aware of the transitory. In the expressive force of its representation and in its symbolism as a memorial, this gravestone from the Ilissos, no less than the stele of Ameinokleia, shows plainly the vanishing of an old certainty.

There is no question that this gravestone has much to say to us, because it touches familiar emotions; but let us climb further, with courageous steps, into earlier centuries. At about Fig. 10 the turn of the fifth century, 400 B.C., we find the stele of Hegeso. Like that of Ameino-

18

10   *Grave stele of Hegeso. Marble. 149 cm. high*

kleia, it takes us into the friendly quiet of the women's chamber. A standing servant hands her seated mistress the jewel case, from which Hegeso takes something with her delicately formed fingers, and examines it critically. By means of a symmetrical arrangement and the contrast of posture, flat areas, motion and drapery, the two female figures are carefully balanced and arranged to make a whole possessing an inner tension as compared to the more uniform effect of the gravestone of Ameinokleia. In the latter a unified mood is varied with gently graduated penetration, but the sculptor of Hegeso's grave relief allowed unlikes to exist side by side, more completely independent from one another. His work contains more action and dialogue than lyric. Formally this is expressed in the contrast between simplicity and variety of posture, narrowness and spaciousness, plain and rich drapery, the simple folds of the servant's closely fitting robe and the intricate flowing of her mistress's drapery, gentle, regular rounding and free fluctuation between light and shadow. Instead of the sorrow of parting, this relief shows a permanent, confident life, still existing. The gazes of the two women still have an attainable goal; they are not dreaming and lost, as the women in the Ameinokleia relief. Life exists and is not called in question.

Fig. 11

A generation earlier, about 430 B.C., a master who had worked on the frieze of the Parthenon created a classic gravestone, which was discovered at Salamis. It was erected for a youth who is portrayed along with his small servant. The youth holds a little bird in his left hand, which hangs at his side, and reaches with his right hand toward an object which cannot be clearly interpreted, probably a cage for a bird or a cricket, both playthings of Greek youth. He bears himself entirely as a living man, secure in his relationship to the actual world. The boy, who is in front of him, is considerably smaller than he, and leans against a grave stele upon which a cat sits, probably a statue crowning it rather than a living animal. The values are curiously displaced: while the youth is meant to be the deceased and the boy a live person, the youth appears as the very image of existing vitality, while the boy in contrast looks weary, dreaming rather than awake. Continuing existence characterizes the youth, while the boy, like the servant on the tombstone from the Ilissos, is troubled in the basis of his existence and seems to lose his grip; compared to the youth, he gives the impression of disappearing. To express the observer's feeling, the form of the small servant brings the shadow of death and sorrow into the bright picture of a life-filled existence which is preserved in the portrait of the youth for whose death the monument was erected. In this work, too, its meaning as a memorial is compressed to the utmost: to preserve, in the symbol which sorrow erects above the deceased, the continuance of his existence. This is characteristically a statue of the great period of classicism because it embraces opposites in its design, and brings conflicting elements into balance in its content.

Fig. 12

A grave stele from the early classic period, called the stele Giustiniani after its former owner, is, in contrast, transparently simple and unequivocal. With a charming gesture, a maiden has taken something from the pyxis which she holds in her left hand, and whose cover lies at her feet, probably grains of incense for an offering to the gods. Like the curve of the cylindrical pyxis, every plastic shape in this rather shallow relief is very smooth in its elevations and indentations, so that light and shade bring out an even plasticity without strong constrasts, and the linear boundary has less weight in comparison. The woolen material of the heavy peplos scarcely allows free play to the body and limbs beneath it, but its rich folds serve as an effective foil for the delicate arm and graceful neck. The masterliness and refinement of the modeling and marble work indicate the Parian school of art, to which we would ascribe this statue in any case, because of its origin on one of the Cyclades. The vivacity of the figure allows nothing of death or the mood of sorrow to show through, such as we feel in the funeral stele of the fourth century, even though here too the figure portrayed is that of the deceased. The lifelikeness of the maiden, who is carrying out a simple act of pious worship, perhaps even honoring the dead, is preserved forever in the natural objectivity of the picture.

11 Grave stele from Salamis. Marble. 110 cm. high.

The fifth century saw the flowering of a type of vessel intended as decoration for graves, the white-ground lekythoi, with pictures that are closely related to the reliefs of the stelae. Their predominant subject matter is the life of women and girls: mistress and servants, maidens in friendly concourse, a mother and nurse with a small child, the warrior parting from his wife. Thus these ceramic grave ornaments, like the pictorial stelae, show the continuance of the simple activities of daily life.

Solitary examples of the stelae can be found beyond the middle of the sixth century, back into the preceding seventh. Insofar as these archaic stelae show pictures in relief, they portray men and boys almost without exception.

12 Grave stele Giustiniani. Marble. 222 cm. high.

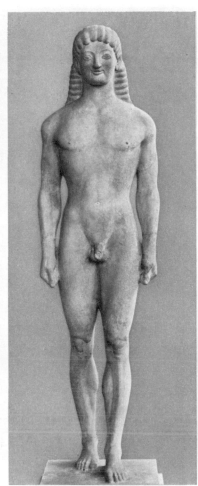

13   Grave stele of Aristion. Marble. 240 cm. high.   *14 and 15   Kouros from Tenea. Marble. 153 cm. high.*

The gravestone of an Attic noble, the stele of Aristion, signed by the sculptor Aristocles, Fig. 13
originated toward the end of the archaic epoch, about 510 B.C. On it, the man who has
died continues his life as a warrior. He wears a helmet on his bearded head, a breastplate
over a finely pleated chiton, and greaves, the careful execution of which reveals the sculptor's
striving to be faithful to reality and anatomically exact. The finely articulated feet and the
convincingly foreshortened left hand, grasping a spear, are masterpieces of clear, graphic
portrayal. Closely bounded by the lateral edges of the slender stone, the warrior is portrayed
in pure profile, facing right.

THIS STELE invites comparison with the portraits of youths in the round from the same century, the archaic kouroi. It gives an impression as if the side view of one of these three-dimensional statues had been thoughtfully translated into flat relief; it corresponds exactly in the erect posture, the balanced stance on both legs, with the left foot placed less than its own length in front of the right, and the right arm bent slightly, with clenched fist. But here we are concerned not merely with a formal resemblance, but also with a corresponding Fig. 14, 15 purpose and meaning. The statue illustrated beside the gravestone of Aristion is also a grave monument, as we know because it was found in a necropolis at Tenea, near Corinth. Sometimes this statue is called the Apollo of Tenea, because the youthful god Apollo was portrayed in the same way, as a perfectly formed, magnificent youth. When neither the circumstances in which it was found, nor an inscribed name, nor definite attributes, such as a bow for Apollo or a piece of athletic equipment for a youth, enables us to interpret one of these ancient statues, we speak of it simply as the 'portrait of a youth,' a kouros; and in thus leaving the identification indefinite, we are following the example of the Greeks themselves, who were notoriously indifferent about the matter. As a healthy ideal of youthful beauty, the young man corresponds to the god Apollo; they are actually of the same nature, and 'the question still remains whether they are gods or men' (Goethe, Faust II). In any case, such a distinction between being and reality in image and form is only a concern of latter-day moderns. The early Greek sculptor created an actual being which, in its existence as an image, towered above time and, in its absolute form, is both god and youth. For a sculptor with such a vocation, the expression that the ancient Egyptians used for their sculptors – namely, those who 'kept alive' – seems particularly applicable. To preserve existence was the task of Greek sculptors of the archaic period, in their grave statues and stelae. They 'always produced life,' said Goethe of the Greek funereal monuments.

In this connection, a story reported by Herodotus is particularly enlightening as an aid to understanding the early Greek point of view. Two youths, Kleobis and Biton, were both distinguished for their remarkable physical strength, and had won many a victory in the gymnastic games. Because oxen were missing, they pulled their mother, a priestess of Hera, in her chariot a great distance to the sanctuary at Argos. For this pious deed, their mother prayed the gods to reward them and, as the greatest boon they could grant, the gods allowed the two brothers to die in their sleep, in the full strength of their youth. To commemorate this occurrence the Argives commissioned their countryman Polymedes to prepare images

24

of Kleobis and Biton. These statues were not placed on their graves; instead, they were consecrated in the Delphic temple of Apollo, where they remain to this day. That youth should not be spoiled by old age, and that the best gift of the ageless gods is to snatch it suddenly away; that the dead youths actually continue to live for all time in the images of them; that the glorious excellence of their statues, which may have been intended for erection on their graves, made them worthy of serving as a votive offering in the divine temple – all this in the story shows how, to the early Greek mind, the most diverse kinds of ideas can be closely allied, inextricably, unconditionally, and without contradiction.

The double group of Kleobis and Biton, which Polymedes of Argos created for the temple Fig. 16 at Delphi about the turn of the seventh century, shows two broad-chested, rather short, muscular youths with powerful legs. Strength at its full, mature vigor is expressed in these portraits, for it shows, as Solon once declared, 'what man is good for.' Facing straight forward, the two statues stand side by side, and are typical of the many portraits of youths that are so frequent in the archaic plastic art of the sixth century. They are distinguished, not by conscious 'art,' but as primary examples of a natural type. Kleobis and Biton appear to be characteristic Argives, sons of the Doric countryside which, according to ancient tradition, is the cradle of classic Doric architecture, and which contributed substantially to the development of plastic art. Compared to the earthy robustness of their firmly knit physiques, the Corinthian kouros of Tenea has a more supple, smoother effect; their joints and muscles are

16 Kleobis and Biton. Marble. 216 cm. high.

25

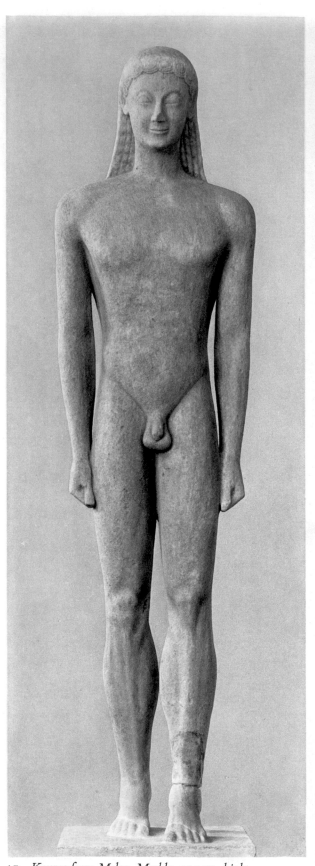

17 *Kouros from Melos. Marble. 214 cm. high.*   18 *Apollo from Piombino. Bronze. 115 cm. high.*

more strongly emphasized, the expression is fresher, and their eyes gaze openly into the world, as we might expect from the scions of a land that carried on worldwide trade.

A third kouros, illustrated here in order to increase our view of the rural types of early Fig. 17 Greece, is the kouros of Melos, approximately contemporary to the statue from Tenea, but from an entirely different source, the Ionian islands. He is slender and delicate, as though he had shot up too fast, and his expression restrained and contemplative, as though, on his distant island, the growing youth had been little touched by the world. If we dare to call any work of plastic art lyrical, this is it, so soft and refined are the flow of the contours and the fusion of trunk and limbs. But no matter how variously each sculptor expresses himself, in his own manner, determined by his innate racial heritage or his ability as an artisan, either restrained or free, crudely or elegantly, angularly or smoothly – still, all the archaic kouroi, from the later seventh to the turn of the fifth century, have a single basic form in common, and present the human figure of the time as a straight, upright, sound, natural, and happy young being. All of these youthful images are nude, not because this was the custom in everyday life or during gymnastic games, but so that their essence may be revealed, undisguised. Because they were intended for similar purposes, Egyptian statues have often been called upon for comparison, but the nude image of the male was very rare among them. That the body, as well as the demeanor, has its 'arete,' its virtue – that strength, health, and beauty are just as important as bravery, righteousness and prudence – is a unique concept of the ancient Greeks. Naked and untouched by false modesty, the early Greek youth is presented as a human being pure and simple, distinguished by nature and molded by education and custom.

These kouroi stand firmly with both feet on the ground, the right leg placed fairly far backward and the left slightly forward. The muscles are tensed in calves, thighs and buttocks. The upper part of the body rises perpendicular and erect. The figure is built up around the central axis of the body as though designed with compass and ruler, both sides the same, every part in balance. The arms hang at the sides, to the middle of the thighs, in the early statues very straight and pressed closely to the body, but later with elbows bent more and more, and forearms extended. The hands, almost without exception, are clenched to make fists, as though the youth were summoning up his strength. The head faces straight forward, and the face is framed by long hair falling over the neck in back. The features are beaming, joyful, alert. What appears to us as a smile expresses a self-confident, secure feeling for life – in early works, naïvely joyful, later more thoughtful, sometimes refined, and finally austere. We hear the echo, clear and meaningful, of words from early archaic lyrics, such as Sappho's, words that are translated by 'smiling' or 'beaming with joy.'

This basic figure of the kouros, when it appears in the brittle material of marble, is strictly oriented to the four primary surfaces of the block of stone. The kouroi in bronze, a more supple and firm material, have a rounder, somewhat more relaxed effect in the posture of the limbs, especially in the freer action of the arms. The late archaic bronze youth of Piom- Fig. 1, 18 bino, in spite of his greater freedom of stance, his strongly angled arms extended forward, and the very supple and articulate rounding of his body and limbs, still has the same basic aspects when viewed from the front or from one of the two sides, preferably the right. The fact that this statue was found on Italian land and has a dedicatory inscription to Athena in the Doric dialect leads us to assume that its original home was a Greek colony in lower Italy, possibly Tarentum. In spite of the archaic modelling of the whole, the details of the work show more developed traits; it may be that a bronze caster here in the colonial area still held firm to the ancient traditions at a time when the early-classic image of the human being had already developed in his motherland, especially in Attica. This bronze kouros is usually called the Apollo of Piombino, but this is probably not a correct interpretation, because it would be difficult to complete the figure with the bow of the far-shooting god in the left hand, and an Apollo would scarcely have served as a votive offering to Athena. That this interpretation lies in the realm of possibility illustrates the essential features of the archaic 'portrait of a youth.'

Fig. 19, 20   On the other hand, an Attic bronze statuette from the Acropolis, dating about 500 B.C., is proved, through the sport gear he once held in his hands, to be a boy who was being trained in the gymnasium. The magnificent little statue shows the greatest possible variation from the basic form of the kouros. The upper body, pushing slightly forward, seems to express an unusual eagerness, as though the boy were on the point of undertaking something, while the older kouroi stand motionless, as though they had been ordered to attention. The stance is somewhat broader and longer, the arms are tensed at an angle, and are relatively far away from the trunk at each side. In profile, the outline of the body displays strong projections, contractions, and intersections. The surface expands and is elaborated in manifold shapes. In the expression of the face, more austere features take the place of the joyful smile; we can, through his alert and lively spirit, recognize in the boy a child of Attica. This masterpiece stands at the borderline of a new epoch, the severe classical, and proclaims a changing humanity.

Fig. 23   The threshold of the classic period of the fifth century is plainly crossed when we consider the marble statue of a boy, which also originated in the Acropolis. It fits into the sequence of early Greek 'portraits of youths,' but has a peculiarly boyish effect in comparison to the eternal essence of youth expressed in the archaic kouroi. This boy has his individual boyishness; he no longer stands in a fore-ordained order of existence as they did, but is independent. His bearing is completely different from that of the archaic kouroi. Instead of being limited by the solid stance, his posture is freer, with the weight of the body born on the left leg, while the right is relaxed, slightly bent and placed to the side. This results in a gentle vivacity of the whole body, a well-balanced freedom of bearing in which the horizontal parts of the trunk are shifted from the true horizontal, and the center line away from the perpendicular axis of the body. The head is turned slightly toward the right, and the gaze seems to have had a self-determined direction. Unfortunately the inlaid eyeballs, made of costly material to lend a shine to the gaze, have been lost from the sockets. They would scarcely have tempered the serious expression of the features, especially around the austere, some-

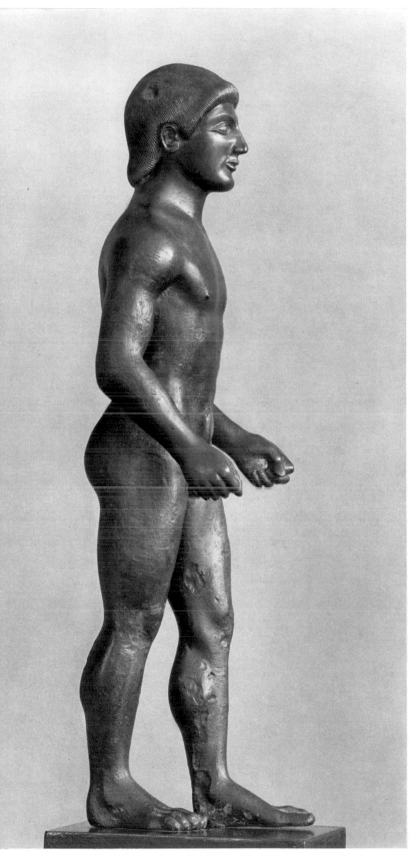 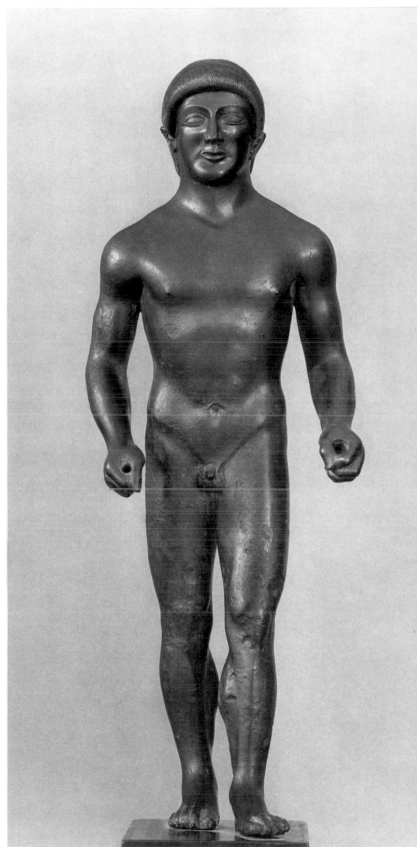

19 and 20   Boy from the Acropolis. Bronze. 27 cm. high.

what reserved, mouth. This boy shows his gradual awakening and increasing self-knowledge in contrast to the cheerful security of the archaic kouroi. There is stirring in him a fore-knowledge of his own capacity to keep his balance and be independent. He is in the years when boys train their bodies and cultivate their minds.

Fig. 21, 22   Similar boys in the palaestra (gymnasium) appear in the painted representations on a white-ground alabastron and a cylindrical cup-holder, the latter the work of an anonymous artist who is called the Antiphon Painter. The four boys pictured are separated from each other by the narrow wall of the vessel, so that only one can be seen at the same time, entirely alone; and because of this, each figure gains something self-reliant, statuesque. They are not presented in lively action, as we will find to be true with the older painters; rather, the boys of the Antiphon Painter stand as calmly as statues. The athletic gear in their hands is only a symbol; the painter is not concerned with narrating achievements, but with portray-ing conduct and sound constitution. The boys of the Antiphon Painter are different from similar older images, not only in their free bearing, but also in a rounder physique. They almost appear to be counterparts physically to the marble statue of the boy of the Acropolis. At that time, both painting and plastic art aimed at a freer rounding of the body, and these

21   *Boy in the Palaestra. Cup-holder by the Antiphon Painter (detail). Clay. Height of the cup, 26.5 cm.*
22   *Boy in the Palaestra. White-ground alabastron (detail). Clay. Height of the vessel, 18 cm.*

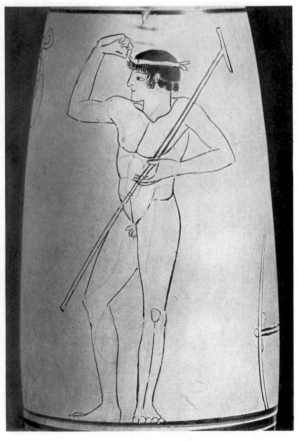

little pictures of the Antiphon Painter, with their linear representation of form, make especially clear what the artists of those decades were concerned with in their picturing of the human figure – something that is not so immediately apparent in the plastic art. The painter avoided the line drawn beautifully for its own sake; the line is a servant of plastic clarification, it makes clearly visible the movements and curves of the body and the tension of the muscles. The archaic calligraphy of abdominal musculature and ribs gives way to stronger lines found exactly in those places where, in the statue, the plastic surface motion is the strongest. Both works must have been made at approximately the same time, and we have definite evidence for dating the marble statue of the boy. The position in which it was discovered, in the 'Persian debris,' indicates that it must have originated shortly before the destruction of the Acropolis by the Persians in the year 480. It is apparently the work of the same sculptor, Critios, who, after the dispersal of the Persians, created a new statue of Harmodius to replace the one in the group of the tyrannicides Harmodius and Aristogiton, the work of Antenor, which had been carried off by the Persians. Therefore the statue, made of beautiful marble, perhaps Parian, is called the Boy of Critios.

The intellectual phases of this boy's training and education are illustrated by pictures on the outside of the cup of Douris, which is approxi-Fig. 24 mately contemporary. It affords insight into the school instruction, the aesthetic rearing, of boys. In the presence of attentive pedagogues, men and youths instruct them in writing, in reading and reciting verses from a scroll, in singing to the accompaniment of a double flute, and in playing

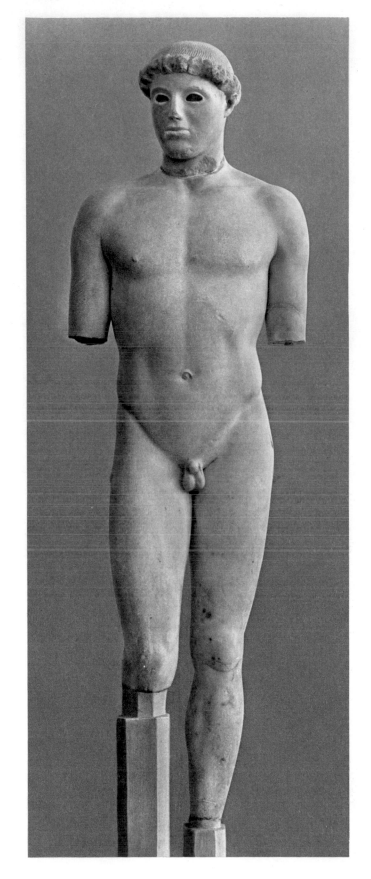

23 Youth by Critios, from the Acropolis. Marble. 86 cm. high.

31

together on the lyre. In addition to cups and a three-legged vessel shown around the edge, there are lyres, a probable tuning fork, a blackboard, and a bundle of slate-pencils to complete the equipment of the school hour. From Greek history we learn that the education of boys was less a matter of learning various sorts of worthwhile facts, and more the development of the capacity for knowledge. It was that of which we still catch a faint echo in our worn-out word 'education' – the bringing forth of conduct fitting an individual in human society. As the music master and boys play the lyre together, it is not so much a question of practicing a piece of music, as assimilating rhythm and harmony. In this way, Plato believed, boys are trained for speaking and acting as true citizens. Plato repeatedly expressed his thoughts about the great significance of music in education. Its importance rested in this, that 'rhythm and harmony sink into the inmost part of the soul and fasten most firmly upon it, bringing gracefulness and making it graceful if one is well trained.' The classical Greek concern for the education of the human being first became a subject for painters at the beginning of the classic epoch, at whose end Plato stood, and Douris managed to give incomparable expression to this 'substance of experienced reality' in his pictures. For, if a picture is to illustrate fittingly the inner meaning of education through rhythm and harmony, then the design of the picture itself must have these attributes. In actual fact, such harmony prevails in the distribution and symmetry of the groups, the balance and variation of the figures, rhythmically placed, so that every component part of the picture fills a definite function in the composition of the whole. The tranquil existence of the figures directs the observer's attention all the more effectively to the relationships between them, and gives them an inner unity.

The increased concern in the fifth century with human education, both gymnastic and aesthetic, corresponded to a new image of the human being in Greek plastic art, and it is appropriate to the new methods of education that the classic 'portraits of youths,' in distinction to their archaic predecessors, are fashioned in a more individual manner. As human society strives to produce the well-rounded individual, the rounded qualities of statues stand forth more clearly. In respect to the plastic quality, the essence lies within the shape. The Fig. 25 statue – for example, the bronze torso of a youth in Florence, from the severe classical period – gives the impression that a life force, surging out from within, fills the pores of the bronze skin to the utmost tension. Rilke felt the same thing when he wrote of a marble torso of about this same period, the early fifth century (not an 'archaic torso of Apollo,' as he called it in his poem), that the stone 'would break out of all its borders like a star.' We must assume that the sculptor's imagination did not see from outside the work that was coming into being, but that instead he became identified with it, transported his mind inside it, and lived his way out of the material with it. It is impossible to express in words that part of artistic accomplishment which must always remain a mystery; but in these works, as distinguished from the modern, we seem to sense that they were brought forth through an inner participation, not by outer manipulation. The result is an inexpressibly new, full state of plastic art that affects us like the flowering of a healthy nature.

32

24 *Education of boys. Outside of a cup by Douris (detail). Clay. Diameter of the cup, 28.5 cm.*

For the head which is lacking on the bronze torso, we may substitute a marble boy's head Fig. 26 which, like that of the Boy of Critios, is dated, by the circumstances in which it was found, before the destruction of the Acropolis by the Persians. To traces of color in his hair, he owes his name 'The Blond Head.' His features do not express the serious alertness and lively vivacity of the Boy of Critios. His gloomier, more heavy-blooded disposition differentiates him from the Attic works, and leads us to think of an Argive sculptor. Here all the shapes are firmer, and the full plasticity is more concise and almost stereometric in comparison to the Boy of Critios. We might call the latter plastic, the former architectonic. In spite of geographical differences, these two statues, like all their contemporaries, have in common a fullness of life springing from a renewed artistic force which is more concerned with truth and simplicity than with the aesthetically pleasing and decorative, in which many of the late archaic works excel.

Among the early works of the severe classical period, the Delphic charioteer occupies an Fig. 28, 29 outstanding place. Polyzalos, the Lord of Gela, presented him as a votive offering in the temple at Delphi some time between 478 and 474. The pillar-like, upright, smoothly draped charioteer is the only remaining part of a great plastic group; there are only a few fragments left of his chariot and the team of four horses with which the celebrated victory in the arena was won. The driver's extended right hand still grasps remnants of the reins. The long, narrow garment tied around the shoulders is his characteristic garb. The head shows a youth of sensuous power and austere features, with a light down of beard at the edge of his cheeks. In this 'portrait of a youth,' the basic figure of the archaic kouros has been abandoned, not only the posture but also the nudity, and into its place has stepped a more exactly identified figure, the youth victorious in a chariot race. Such closer identifications are now customary. Myron's discus-throwing youth belongs in the same category.

Fig. 27 Images of gods and of men are now also more definitely differentiated. The bronze statue raised from the sea near Cape Artemision in 1928 must represent a god, probably Poseidon, if one assumes correctly that he once held a trident in his right hand. That the statue surpasses usual human dimensions is not a determining factor; it is rather that this work expresses a sublimity that transcends all concepts of the human being. The majestic physique, the elastic, springing pose, the bold extension of the arms denote the mighty ruler of earthly realms and natural forces, and the head reveals the divine eminence of the figure. When this 'god from the sea' was created around the middle of the fifth century, probably by an unknown Attic master, Phidias was already at work, the sculptor whom the ancients considered their most important maker of gods. He was able to fashion, as no other artist could, the sublimity and dignity of the gods, those gods of ancient Greece who are, above all, the Gods of Homer. For Phidias' statue of Zeus in Olympia, the ancients found no higher praise than to say that it embodied the verses of Homer.

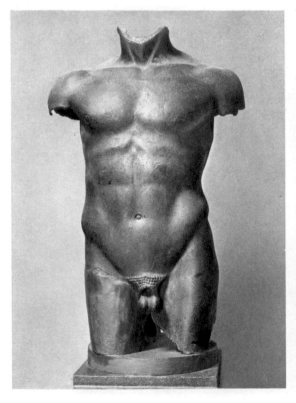

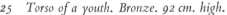

25   *Torso of a youth. Bronze. 92 cm. high.*   26   *'Blond Head' from the Acropolis. Marble. 25 cm. high.*

34

27 *Poseidon from Cape Artemision. Bronze. 209 cm. high.*

28 and 29   Charioteer. Bronze. 180 cm. high.

36

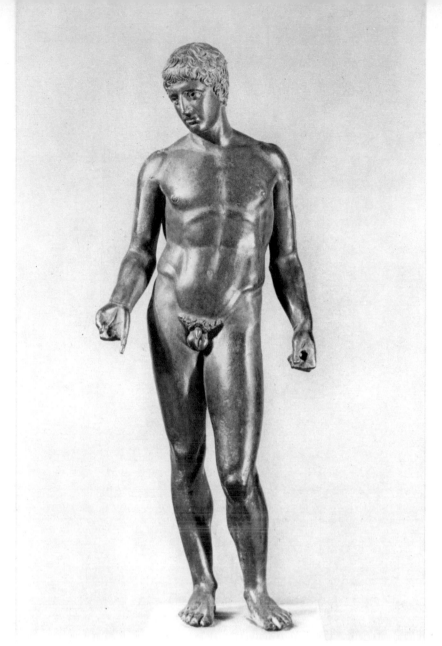

30 *Youth. Bronze. 21 cm. high.*
31 *Youth. Bronze. 21 cm. high.*

POLYKLETOS

WE HAVE unexpectedly arrived again at the height of the classic period, and have turned from the 'portraits of youths' to images of men and gods. Let us return once more to the statues of youths, for the most significant Greek sculptor, next to Phidias, of the high classical period in the third quarter of the fifth century, Polykletos, applied his powers to this very thing. We can no more illustrate a work definitely ascribed to him by tradition than we

39

Fig. 30, 31

can a work by Phidias. Their famous works have been lost in the original, and there remain only copies of a few of them, particularly from the time of the Roman Caesars. We shall include none of these copies, whose excellence varies, in this limited selection of Greek masterpieces, because, in face of the uniqueness of inner and outer form, it is as impossible for a copy to reproduce the superior individuality of the original creation as it is to translate a poetic work into a foreign language. Instead of such copies, two bronze statuettes of youths from the high classic period may be appropriate to convey a glimpse of the Polykletian style.

Polykletos, so we are told, worked primarily in bronze; indeed, he brought the art of molding bronze to the heights of perfection. In his portrayals he is said to have avoided the more mature ages, and did not go beyond smooth cheeks; and he is said to have fashioned his statues so that they appeared to stand on one leg. This statuary motive, attributed to Polykletos as a novelty, is shown in the two bronze statuettes: it is the emphatic differentiation between the leg on which the figure stands and the leg that takes no weight. The right leg, with the foot flat, stands under the figure's center of gravity and bears with full force the mighty trunk, while the left, almost free of weight, is placed back and to one side. This counterpoise gives tension to the quiet stance of the figure, and the trunk is plastically rich in motion, as a consequence of the distribution of weight among its parts and the play of muscles. The position of the arms and turning and inclination of the head do their part to distribute the weight and compensate by counterweight. The functioning of the human organism is in this manner made evident, although the figure remains a genuine statue, self-contained and at rest.

All this has more significance than merely that of a statuary motive or an artistic form, which are frequently used to exhaustion in advanced periods of art. It expresses a true conception of man as a whole, which can fittingly be called 'bearing,' a word with two meanings, which connotes the idea of the Greek classic period that there is a harmony between bearing one's body well and conducting oneself properly, between physical soundness and inner discipline. The Greek word used to designate this type of excellence is difficult to translate: καλοκἀγαθία, the beautiful-good. In portraits of youths during the height of the classic period, this excellence was interpreted differently from the way it was in the archaic kouroi. A higher order seems to dominate the kouroi completely, and their form seems to be determined by a prescribed, firm ordering of the world and life, the archaic cosmos; while the classic youths have an inner force, an individual ability to be themselves, as shown in their bearing. Polykletos created the statue of a boy who was placing the victor's wreath on his own head. It is deeply significant that here the victor is not honored by the bestowing of the laureal wreath or fillet by Nike or a third person, but that instead he himself carries out the wreathing, as a symbolic expression of the fact that he himself achieved the laurels through his proficiency in the agon. It is equally significant that no arrogance is evident in the boy's action; instead, a quiet modesty prevails, the 'aidos' of the Greeks, which is at the same time deference before the gods. The victor owes his success to them, and to them he gives an image of himself, as a votive offering for their temple. This wonderful flight of Polykletian invention may also be seen in one of the two bronze statuettes illustrated: that of a youth with modestly inclined head, who probably held a discus in his left hand as a symbol of his victory, and, with his right hand, extended in the direction in which he is looking, offers a gift to the gods. Fig. 31

Among Polykletos statues of youths, the ancients praised in particular that of Doryphoros, the spear-bearer, because of its symmetry, the measured relationships of its physical structure, the well-calculated harmony of the limbs in relation to one another and to the whole. Polykletos also wrote a theoretical work about the proportions and symmetry of the human body which, along with the statue of Doryphoros, became the accepted canon. 'The success of a work of art,' reads a quotation from it, 'comes about through many numerical relationships, in the process of which a trifle tilts the balance.' Thus Polykletos belongs in the company of great artists who, like Leonardo da Vinci, sought to discover the bases of excellence in art.

This leads us to the question of whether our concept of the artist is adequate when applied to Polykletos, and whether the idea of the 'artistic' is valid at all for the Greeks. If we go by what we learn about the plastic arts from Greek literature, especially the Greek philosophers, we must conclude that their opinion was basically different from the high esteem we give to art and the artist in modern times. We should not be led astray by the word '*techne*,' which was used to designate the work of the plastic artist, as well as the dexterity of the artisan and expertness in all kinds of mechanical and intellectual fields, and we should not think solely of its derivative, 'technique.' In its fullest meaning, it encompasses both the idea of a professional facility that can be acquired, and the idea of inspiration and the intellectual, with the former by no means outweighing the latter. Aristotle, on the threshold of Hellenism, first recognized 'a spiritual element in the fabricating process in art and handicraft,'[2] but his observation is still based 'completely on the classical equating of art and handiwork, and excludes the concept of the creative.' When we consider what an important part the '*paideia*' – the contribution of all intellectual accomplishments to the shaping of the human being – played in Greek thought, it is all the more surprising that, according to what has come down to us in writing, 'it never occurred to a Greek to concede a place in the *paideia* to plastic art or its contemplation,'[3] since to us it appears that nothing reveals so unmistakably the well-formed human being as the statue at the height of the classic period. Perhaps the work of the plastic artist is too far removed from pure thought to be included, because the latter aims at logical and universal concepts, the former at visible images. 'He who wants to understand the artist,' says Goethe, 'must go into the artist's land.'

In mythology, the 'pre-philosophical cosmos of the Greeks,'[2] we already find an important distinction between the various manifestations of what, in more recent times, is called the artistic spirit. Poetry and music were cultivated by Apollo and were ascribed to the inspiration of the Muses. The Iliad and the Odyssey begin with invocations to the Muses, Hesiod describes his vocation to be a writer as an awakening by the Muses, and in the Odyssey it says of the singer Demodocos, 'The god gave to him the fullness of song.' Artistic skill, plastic creativity, weaving, and forging belong to the province of Athena and Hephaistos. Hephaistos fabricates all sorts of costly vessels for the domestic life of the gods and, Fig. 100 at the request of the goddess Thetis, forges a shield for her son Achilles. Athena is shown on a vase in the act of molding a horse, but this is probably a very unusual and significant work, the Trojan horse with which the destruction of Troy began. While the mythical singers, Linos, Orpheus, or Amphion, were said to be sons or apprentices of the gods, ancient mythology seems to know nothing of a bronze sculptor, a goldsmith, or a potter who might have been the son of a god or who had taken lessons from a divine being. If Socrates once called the fabulous Daedalus his ancestor, and a successor of Apollo, the philosopher did so only to symbolize his belief that he was divinely commissioned in his effort to shape men. It is true that in mythology the plastic arts are not excluded from the realm of divine activity, but they are no more derived from divine inspiration than they are in Aristotle. Hephaistos, the real artist among the Olympian gods, is a shabby fellow who is laughed at and treated disdainfully when he limps into their company. This mirrors the position of the sculptor and artisan in society: they are rated extraordinarily low, and rank with the Thetans, 'who are indeed free, but do slave labour for wages.'[4] It was not until the more modern intellectual concepts of Hellenism that a higher evaluation of artistic creation became established, and even then the artist was not granted social recognition.

The circumstances appear in a somewhat different light when we enter the 'artist's land' itself. As the centuries move forward, more and more artists are known to us by name. Artists' inscriptions begin in the early seventh century with the signature of the potter Callicles; toward the end of the same century, the first sculptor signed his name on a pedestal in Delos, Euthycartides the Naxian. In this way, the 'individuality of the person'[5] began at the start of the archaic epoch, and this is true of names in general as well as the signatures of artists. The number of artists' names remains scanty during the first half of the sixth century; but a masterpiece of this period, a splendid crater, is signed both by the potter Ergotimos and by the painter Klitias (Fig. 71, 72). After the middle of the century artists' inscriptions increase substantially, especially those of potters and vase painters, but also occasionally of sculptors. The self-confident pride of a vase painter and his rivalry are expressed when he adds to a picture: 'Euthymides made it, as Euphronios never could.' After the fifth century, not only do written sources flow more fully with news of plastic artists, but reflections on art also begin to play a larger role than before. In a manuscript by the musician Damon, he is concerned, in addition to the practice of his art, with the theory of music. The somewhat more recent philosopher Democritus, who was experienced in many skills, wrote a dissertation 'On Painting.' We hear of a philosophical conversation between Socrates, the painter Parrhasius, and a sculptor. Phidias apparently represented the artist personality on a higher level of freedom than the lowly and limited position of the artisan, for he was not only trusted with an unusually important task, the total direction of all the work of reconstructing the Acropolis, but also was honored with the personal friendship of the leading statesman Pericles. Here, too, Polykletos has his historical place. How can it be more exactly determined?

We learn no more of his circumstances of life than that he was considered an Argive by some and a Sicyonian by others, and that he stood at the peak of his activity around 420–417. However, we are concerned not with the biographical, but with the artistic personality of Polykletos. For this, the information that he also set down some basic reflections about his art is of importance. He wanted not only to exercise his art, but also to understand it. When we remember that Socrates, at about the same time, was seeking an understanding of virtue, we realize that Polykletos' search for an understanding of art was in the spirit of the times. It represented more than the professional knowledge of an artisan, and was a decisive step toward artistic self-knowledge, leading toward the future. Polykletos sought to establish the regular laws that govern the structure of the human figure, and in this he aimed at finding the prototype which lies at the basis of every human being. It was to serve as the rule, the canon for his representation of the human figure. The Polykletian concept of the canon as paradigm (model or pattern) has been convincingly correlated with the general concepts of Plato, the Platonic Ideas.[6] For Polykletos, the canon was not a generalization derived from observations of reality, the form in which it appears among more recent and modern artists; rather, it meant seeing through the actual into what lies at the basis of it. This helps us to understand a saying handed down concerning Lysippos, the important bronze caster at the end of the fourth century, who pointed to the Doryphoros of Polykletos as his master. Lysippos is supposed to have said that the ancients had fashioned men 'as they are,' while he, on the contrary, made them 'as one descries them.' If we claim for Polykletos this characteristic of the ancients, which distinguishes their work from the realism of Lysippos, it may mean that Polykletos adhered to the absolute being. This, finally, may be the sense of Quintilian's observation that Polykletos made his human figures 'super-real.'

Now the artistic nature of Polykletos, about which we are inquiring, appears in a special light. The archaic sculptors of the kouroi have their place in a fixed order. They bring into concrete existence a preordained basic figure, using all the means at their command, and do not arbitrarily change it. What we call invention of motif or artistic object was not up to the sculptor's own judgment. This makes clear to what an extent the sculptor of that period counted simply as a workman, for what he needed was proficiency, learned 'techne', and skill of hand, to objectify an ideal prototype. In Polykletos, this bond with a traditional order has been loosened, but he has by no means become a freely creative artist. He himself seeks to discern the prototype, the absolute being of the human figure, in order again to be governed arbitrarily by this model. He was never his own master in invention and in following realism to the same degree that the more recent Lysippos was. Compared with the latter, Polykletos' portraits of youths are as a rule amazingly alike. They are differen-

tiated by different 'ideas': whether it be the young boy, the boy in whom the first signs of manhood are burgeoning, or the youth, the spear-bearer, the victor who is bandaging his head or placing the laurel wreath on it – or even an occasional supernatural being of mythology, such as Achilles. Polykletos is neither an artisan in the old sense nor a creative artist in the modern; the scales within him hold both in balance. But soon, and more and more in Hellenism, the balance will tip toward the artist. It is a great moment in the history of what we call art. It has already become clear (and will be confirmed again) that we should simply avoid speaking of art, as far as practicable, in connection with the Greeks. Instead of writing a history of Greek art, one might better attempt to trace the coming into being of art itself among the Greeks.

BURIAL CUSTOMS AND THE CULT OF THE DEAD AS THE ORIGIN OF ART

WE HAVE wandered far from our starting point, the portraits of youths on the archaic grave stelae, and now must resume again our observation of sculpture intended to honor the dead, in order to penetrate even farther back into Greek antiquity. The slender grave stelae with human figures in relief are preceded by older ones without such pictures. The most conscientious of them are decorated with incised patterns and borders, but the older are merely roughhewn, oblong stones of moderate size, occasionally bearing a name. The name identifies the stone unmistakably with the dead, it assumes his place, and gravestones have been called the 'souls of the dead.' Similarly, we learn from Homer that, when a companion of Odysseus lost his life, the oar he used was planted as a symbol on the mound over his grave; and in other parts of Homer's poem we read of the stone, the stele, being used as a grave marker. This makes it easier for us to understand why the early grave reliefs held so fast to life, preserved so strongly the reality of the deceased: they are proxies.

The century of Homer opens up before us, and with it, the great early age of the geometric style. The largest quantity of what has been preserved for us from that age comes from burial places, especially the productive necropolises of Athens, the cemeteries in the Fig. 32 area of the more recent Agora, or near the Dipylon and the Sacred Gate, on roads which lead from the center of the city to the harbor of Piraeus or the sacred Eleusis. The ceramic products served the purpose of concealing bones and ashes of the dead, and sometimes the whole bodies of children. Large urns were closed with smaller vessels, in place of the older stone covers. Variously shaped small vessels were cremated along with the dead and added to the contents of the urns in the pit. Votive vessels were placed on the mounds. The stone monument was a later addition. Instead of clay urns, costly boxes were sometimes used for the ashes, made of wood inlaid with richly decorated plates of gold. Rediscovered graves where uncremated corpses were buried contain a large number of clay vessels of various sizes; the grave of a woman concealed numerous ceramic jewel boxes, the lids of which, Fig. 33 in several cases, had miniature figures of horses as handles. Ivory statuettes, golden headbands, and bronze drapery pins were deposited in the graves as parting gifts for the dead. All this has meaning and significance with reference to funereal beliefs and the cult of the dead. In many places religion began with the cult of the dead, long before any divine being had assumed tangible shape; and from this essential starting point, we must seek to understand the early products of the Greeks' artistic endeavors. For the early Greeks, as for us, the shocking incomprehensibility of death was one of the strongest experiences of life, and in this zone they first expressed themselves creatively. In these early epochs of the geometrical style, the heritage of Greek culture can be completely understood only in the context of the cult of the dead.

The beginning date of the development of art among the Greeks is set by the Dorian campaign of conquest in the Peloponnesus, which started around 1200 B.C., struck the

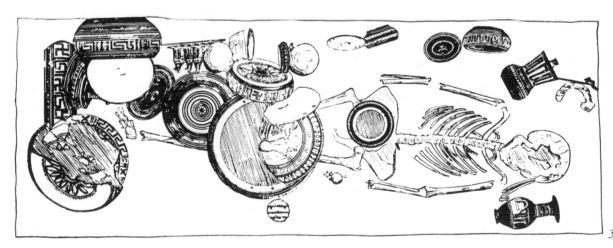

33   *Body grave. Athens, Agora.*

Argolis about the middle of the twelfth century, and led to the destruction of Mycenae about 1100. Athens was not conquered at that time, and was not overwhelmed by the Dorian tribes that were migrating southward. Therefore these tribes were not responsible for bringing the new spirit of which we find the richest evidence on the ground of Athens. But the immense upheaval taking place all around was not without effect in Athens too. With great exertion, she had to ward off the surging folk migrations. Achaean fugitives from the Peloponnesus sought refuge in Athens and indirectly brought with them the vicissitudes of the migration. Transformations had to take place, defensive forces had to be rallied. The legend of Theseus and his uniting of Athens expresses the memory of a rallying of the community in the early epoch about which history is still dark. Theseus became the mythical founder and hero of the city and still has a sacred precinct in the market of Athens, north of the Acropolis.

An inner renewal in warding off destruction, a freeing and strengthening of the life force – thus the Greeks' own spiritual drives, and not an external doom coming from the migration tribes – caused the new beginning and laid the foundations for the abundance of the future. From homely seeds of great natural germinative power, it sprouts slowly, unfolds leaf by leaf and branch by branch, grows sturdy, and through the centuries becomes a tall, stately tree, strong against all storm – Greek culture, which took the place of the ancient so-called Helladic culture that ended with the Mycenaean epoch.

34 *Protogeometric cup. Clay. 10 cm. high.*

35 *Protogeometric amphora. Clay. 44 cm. high.*   36 *Protogeometric amphora. Clay. 47.2 cm. high.*

GEOMETRIC CERAMICS AND VASE PAINTING

Cᴇʀᴀᴍɪᴄ products are the oldest things on which our knowledge of the Greeks is based. The new development does not strike our eyes immediately as something completely different. The craft of pottery remains the same. Vessels had been made in Greece, from about 2300 B.C., on the potter's wheel; and decorating them with paintings in glazed primary colors on a clay ground was an old traditional custom. Still, certain forms of vessels, such as the characteristic Mycenaean ring jugs and smooth cups with tall feet, disappear, as do certain of the patterns, such as pictures of vegetable and animal life, which had already become stiff and stunted in the final phases of Mycenaean culture. The new vase painters hit on pure geometrical forms. From them, the first epoch of Greek art gets its name, the epoch of the protogeometric and of the geometric style. On amphorae of the tenth century, the

Fig. 35, 36

47

protogeometric idiom is already highly developed. The earliest Greek vase painters tried to reduce all linework to its simplest basic forms, the straight and circular line. Thus, at the earliest stage of Greek plastic art, we find revealed an essential of the Greek spirit, the inclination to dissect 'to the last, indivisible (that which can no longer be divided) unit,' 'atomism,' the 'segmenting force of radical systematics.' These quotations, taken from *Die Meisterung der Schrift bei den Griechen (Mastery of Script among the Greek)*,[7] also apply to the beginnings of their ornamentation, and indicate clearly the similarity of their expressions in writing and in images. As words are built up from letters, so the decorative motifs of protogeometric vessels are built up from straight and circular lines in various combinations: horizontal and vertical parallels, lattice networks of intersecting straight lines, zig-zag parallels, chess-board patterns, hatched and latticed triangles, concentric circles, half-circles and quarter-circles. These motifs, constructed from the basic units, are arranged thoughtfully,

Fig. 34   according to laws of sequence, alternation and symmetry. Even in this early period, there is a fondness for groups of motifs with three or more members, the embryonic form of what, centuries later, came to be a characteristic part of the Doric temple, the elaborated triglyph. The phenomenon of protogeometric ornamentation is significant in several respects. It leads us to surmise that some day the Greeks would lay the groundwork of geometry. It reveals an unusual imaginative power of expressing a great deal with simple means. And finally, it shows us that art, in its beginnings, was not derived from an imitation of nature; that, at least in the case of the Greeks, it began with non-objective forms of expression. With these beginnings, the Greeks themselves brand as a lie their later theory about the imitation of nature, mimesis. In history both phenomena stand side by side. A geometric or non-objective art grows concrete and is 'naturalized' in an evolution lasting hundreds of years – only at the end to become again more and more abstract. In its last phases, Mycenaean plant and animal ornamentation had become almost pure pattern. The protogeometric form textures appeared as a fresh beginning, in opposition to these abstracted forms of a nature-imitation that had long been neglected.

The geometric style – using the phrase to designate an epoch – which followed the proto-

Fig. 37, 38   geometric in about 900 B.C., holds fast to segmented geometric units. Some protogeometric motifs were retained at first, such as concentric circles. But now a white axle-cross in the black center is favored, showing an increasing sense of direction and order. The leitmotif, by means of which we chiefly distinguish the geometric style from the protogeometric, is the meander. Although it can be shown to have existed very much earlier, what the Greeks make out of it is an independent Greek accomplishment. The classic hooked meander is the geometric equivalent of the counterpoise of the classical statues: the height of the geometric period is the first Greek 'classic.' With the simplest means, and in the most restricted space, the meander imprisons the utmost in tension and expansion. It scans like the rhythm of a rich, varied verse form: long, medium long, long, short, medium short,

37 *Geometric belly-handled amphora.*
   Clay. 73 cm. high.

38 *Geometric neck-handled amphora.*
   Clay. 50 cm. high.

short, then beginning again with long, and continuing as before. In this measured, forward-moving rhythm, countermovement is added to movement, until it is hard to figure out in which direction the motion proceeds. Although the meander has the potentiality of encircling a vessel completely and closing to form a ring – thus of being without beginning or end, completely self-contained – at the same time, it is full of an uncommon dynamic force. 'Know what rhythm holds men in its bonds,' the lyric poet Archilochos said in the middle of the seventh century, several decades after the geometric method of decoration had come to an end. This sentence expresses the great importance that the Greeks attributed to rhythm as a standard of life, and it reveals a conception of rhythm completely different from our own. 'Here rhythm is the very thing which imposes barriers, stability on motion, the flood.'[8] The texture of the classical meander is to be understood in the same sense.

A Dipylon amphora from the eighth century, a meter and a half high, shows the manifold possibilities for development within the scope of the meander. A simple hooked meander is here worked out in continually richer, more complicated forms. Beginning with the primary

Fig. 39

49

form of the pointed meander, three progressive stages of elaboration follow one another up to just below the handles; further up it is repeated, reversed, made even more complicated; and finally the classic main theme is once again simply executed. A plain pattern of sets of stripes in threes, with a chain of diamonds between them, frames the sequence uniformly and ties it together. The clarity and rhythmic arrangement of the pattern on this amphora show such perfection that we wonder whether the dimensions of the stripes and bands, their height and their intervals, are determined by pure proportions such as prevail in Poly-kletos' canon or the classic form of the Doric temple.

Fig. 40   In the course of the ninth and eighth centuries, the manifold possibilities inherent in geo-metric patterns were tried out and varied with great inventive spirit. Faceted stars and swastikas were added to the basic motifs. Toward the end, the geometric textures show a weakening of imagination. Powerful constrasts of pattern and tense rhythmic textures were avoided; aiming for greater regularity and unity, the artist tried to adapt the forms and groupings of the pattern to one another. Narrow groups of short, oblique, tortuous lines brought about a picturesque agitation. This phenomenon, typical of a decadent period, has been appropriately labeled the 'flicker style,' and is spoken of as a baroque of the geometric style.[9] To the encompassing historical view, the baroque, as well as the classic, is not a one-time phenomenon, but something that returns frequently in the evolution of the artistic spirit. It aspires beyond geometrical austerity and constraint, and an energetic, enterprising younger generation of painters soon aims at freer development.

Like the painters, the potters also go their own way during the epoch of the geometric style; the softness and indefiniteness of outline of the Mycenaean ceramics is no longer an appropriate means of expression for them. They are concerned with more austere and un-mistakable vessel shapes, which are in the same spirit as the patterns. The circular form, which was so important under the protogeometric patterns, and which lies in the very nature of the vessel as it is formed on the potter's wheel, determined the vessel's silhouette

Fig. 36   at that time. The contours of the predominantly black protogeometric amphora illustrated give the impression that it was composed with mathematical exactitude out of convex and concave arcs. The side ears are set especially low on this belly-handled amphora, and at the widest curve of the belly, so that they encroach as little as possible on the pure arc. That is why the spherical shape has such a powerful, compact effect. The high, wide neck is like a separate piece, very clearly set off from the self-contained curves of the belly, as though the two parts had been joined, rather than one developed from the other. Convex and concave shapes here intentionally meet one another abruptly. They are component parts, each with its own importance, which join one another to make a whole.

Fig. 37   The geometric belly-handled amphora with white axle-crosses in circular disks is, for all the crystalline clarity of its outline, more freely shaped. The greatest width of the belly's curve is higher up. Here are the ears, as before, but now they are placed in such a manner

39 Geometric belly-handled amphora from the Dipylon. Clay. 155 cm. high.

that they seem to be conscious of the vessel's gravity. Then the shoulders are rounded in more decisively. The slenderer neck, with a wider and more clearly defined mouth, shows its function more plainly. The changed relationship of the parts bring a rhythmic expression to this egg-shaped amphora which is lacking in the spherical protogeometric amphora. This rhythm is emphasized by the thoughtful graduation and distribution of the encircling bands, as well as by the rich strips of decoration between the ears and around the neck, in which the weighty metope section between the handles is purposely contrasted with the simple meander circle around the neck.

Fig. 38   While this belly-handled amphora represents the severe stage of the geometric style, the more recent neck-handled amphora from around 800 illustrates its maturity. Just as the intricate meanders were added to the simple one here, so too the body of the vessel is constructed in more stages, and they are differently linked together. The handles, which connect the neck and belly, are the decisive factor in giving this impression. They were not merely added because handles are necessary; they fit in as an essential support for the shape. For all its clarity of form, the contour is no longer the guiding factor; instead, the vessel, rounded according to the laws of corporeality, works itself out more plastically. This striking plasticity stands in conjunction with a further developed feeling for the whole organism, as an articulated structure of powerful component parts, such as foot, body, head, shoulder, neck, lip and handle. Especially expressive are the handles for carrying the vase, which begin in the tension-zone of the shoulder and rise sharply from there to form a secure support for the high wall of the neck. Protogeometric absolute form has been replaced by a shape that is full of character and necessary in itself.

Fig. 40   With late-geometric amphorae, and also with the great jugs derived from them, organic articulation of the structure gives way to a greater smoothness of the whole and a lighter

40   *Geometric jug. Clay. 69 cm. high.*

flexibility of the parts. There is a strong shift in the proportions of the parts in relation to one another. The belly, the actual container, must share its function with the neck. The handle of the jug has to have two props, because the material cannot perform what the shape demands. The joining between trunk and neck is slurred over, rather than emphasized. Frequently tortuous bulges are added on shoulder, handle, and mouth, bringing in too much of the plastic; for it is a plasticity of additions, rather than of the substance, as compared to the mature geometric amphorae. Variety and voluptuousness of form take their place beside the restless flickering of the pattern when the baroque moment arrives.

We are no longer accustomed to regard pots as evidences of higher culture and, in distinction to art, we count them at best as handicraft. Nevertheless they are spurs to higher culture, because art – at first instinctive, and later self-conscious art, which is a distinguishing activity of men – is established with vessels from the shaping hand. And not only that: in the case of the Greeks they count, for many centuries, as the most important of their intellectual productions, not only because of their painting, but also as pottery. They are, as we have said, the oldest, and at times the only, products of the Greek hand known to modern man. Here too, at the very beginning, we find that on which our knowledge of ancient cultures is chiefly based. Characteristically, in art as in other fields, the Greeks begin with the elemental; in all their creations, the origin is never denied. In the famous faïences and porcelains since the Renaissance, the original, elemental value has long since been squandered; the nature of the vessel itself is no longer taken seriously. They are *objets d'art*, refined handiwork, intended to be used as wall decoration, show pieces, for the display of paintings – far removed from the useful utensil. Of course, the outstanding masterpieces of Greek pottery were not in everyday use either; nevertheless, there was no general distinction between everyday and festive or solemn use. In the good periods, they were never merely superfluous ornaments. As vessels, for example, it was the same cup you drank out of at the symposium that you gave as a parting gift in the grave of a dead friend, or that you dedicated to the god in a temple.

This elemental factor in Greek ceramics accounts for the fact that the various types of vessels remain clearly defined throughout the centuries. The shape that was successful in a material suited to it, that proved to be sensible and well adapted to its purpose, was not voluntarily changed, but was retained from the beginning on: the amphora for carrying and storing wine and oil; the hydria for fetching water; the crater for mixing; the cylix, the cup, for drinking, as well as the scyphos, the bowl; the aryballos for ointment, and so on. For centuries these family classifications of Greek vessels remained unmixed, and an amphora of the middle fifth century still bears the honored features of its ancestor from the tenth century.

Still another unique feature of Greek vessels is revealed when we compare them to others. The pronounced substantiality of vessels, as we find them among the Greeks, is not at all a thing to be taken for granted. There can be various ideas of what a vessel is: for one person, that which holds is the important thing; another may be more interested in its potentiality for holding. The masters of Chinese Sung ceramics, for example, had a great gift for making the empty hollow of the vessel effective. These potters, like the painters in ink of the same period, were Taoists and treasured the words of Lao-tse: 'One shapes clay and makes a vessel of it: the usefulness of the vessel depends on the nothingness inside.' We could hardly imagine concepts so diametrically opposed as those of the Chinese and the Greeks. In a Chinese ink painting, the essential thing is the incomprehensible between the objects; in a Greek vase painting, the essence appears in the objects themselves. For the not-appearing, which was the beginning of everything for Lao-tse, the Greeks had little susceptibility. Their views were directed toward the solidity and coherence of the existing, in the sense of Parmenides. Dimensions, tangible objectivity and solid substantiality mark Greek vessels. With them begin the plastic works of the Greeks, the greatest of plastic artists.

The great majority of all protogeometric and geometric ceramics have been discovered, as we have said, in necropolises. In vessels, which are lasting and noble by virtue of their material, shape, and ornamentation, what is left of mortal men is preserved. The very first use of vessels as storage containers cannot be imagined apart from this custom. Clear traces of this can still be seen at a time when the religious beliefs of the Greeks were highly developed, and have been pointed out by Nilsson in his researches into Greek religious history.[10] Hades, lord over the realm of the dead, is also called Pluto and this is connected with the literal meaning of Pluto, wealth. Pluto is he who 'had wealth,' and he is lord of the underworld because he is the one to whom everything, and everyone, comes home, who inherits the greatest supplies. On a white-ground lekythos from the classical period, this underworld is represented as a gigantic storage vessel. Hermes, the escort of the dead, is standing in front of it and endeavors to banish within it the souls of the dead that are fluttering around. We could not find a clearer representation of the cycle of relationships between the vessel and storage, funeral urns, the resting place of the dead, and Hades-Pluto.

Fig. 32   The cremation of the dead and the burying of their ashes, for which the protogeometric amphorae served, arrived in Athens directly after the Doric migration, and were the general custom in the protogeometric necropolis near the Dipylon. In the preceding Mycenaean culture, bodies were buried unburned. Thus, at that time there occurred a significant change in the manner of burials, as well as in other things, a change that cannot be explained merely by the customs which the advancing tribes brought with them. The underlying causes for this changed outlook are still unknown. Cremation did not remain prevalent throughout the centuries of this early epoch. With the period of the geometric style, toward the end of

Fig. 33   the ninth century, burials of corpses appear again, and from then on burials and cremations are found side by side. When, at the beginning of the Peloponnesian war (431 B.C.), the plague raged among the population crammed into Athens, and even Pericles fell victim to it, the approaching Spartans saw the smoke of funeral pyres rising over the city, and the fear of contagion caused them to retreat.

54

Homer's Iliad, from the later eighth century, knows only cremation of the dead. In Book XXIII the funeral of Patroklos is described in detail, and from it we can gain a clear idea of the customs of the time. Throughout the night the mighty pile of wood, the trunks of great trees, burned, and not only were animals slaughtered on it as a sacrifice for the dead, but twelve young Trojans also fell as tragic human sacrifices. In the morning the glow was extinguished with wine, and the remains of Patroklos' bones were gathered from the ashes and wrapped in a purple cloth or a finely embroidered fabric. Tatters of such a cloth for the bones have been preserved in a bronze urn from the later fifth century. When gifts are found in protogeometric amphorae, along with the ashes of the dead, we are reminded of the description in the Iliad, which tells us that jugs of honey and oil were placed on the bier and cremated too. The urn was sunk in a pit, covered with a stone or small vessel, then what was left from the cremation, ashes and charred earth, was shaken over it, and a shallow mound piled on top as a mark. Finally the dead man had come to rest; for, as long as Patroklos was still unburied, his psyche, exactly like the living man in size, countenance, and voice, and clothed as he was, appeared to his friend Achilles in dreams, and begged to be buried soon so that he might walk through the gates of Hades and never return.

We have already spoken of the simple gravestones erected above the heap of earth, out of which the pictorial stelae developed, and we have briefly mentioned the setting up of large vessels. The great Dipylon amphora illustrated belonged to such a grave. Some of these Fig. 39, 41 vessels have proved to be dispensers. Their base was perforated so that the liquid offering could penetrate downward and reach the dead. Thus they were not only monuments or decorations for the grave, but served the cult of the dead. This special significance becomes even clearer when stones are erected next to them on the graves. The most important of these vessels are large craters on raised feet more than a meter high. It was on these grave Fig. 42 vessels that pictures of the human figure, rich in content, were developed, sometimes in the circumscribed area between the handles of an amphora, between geometric ornaments, and sometimes in several circular friezes commanding the whole wall of a crater.

The use of figures as motifs along with the geometric patterns came relatively late and, at first, slowly. A few isolated little horses on amphorae of the mature protogeometric period are the first figure-paintings of the Greeks. We would like to think that these small horse pictures are not merely decorative motifs, but have a deeper significance, because at one time the horse symbolized the nobility of the leading social class of Homer's time. In later times, horses still had a special significance in funeral rites. At Patroklos' funeral, Achilles cast four noble steeds on his friend's pyre, as his special gift to the dead. Was the horse perhaps a sacrifice especially appropriate for a cavalier who had died, just as pictures of horses frequently appeared on tripods used as prizes in knightly tournaments? The protogeometric Fig. 35 amphora illustrated shows one of the first horse pictures, in a disadvantageous position beneath the wavy free-hand lines near the ear. The little horse is also drawn free-hand, but with severe, almost geometrical lines; the outlines of the belly and neck are almost perfect arcs.

Fig. 38, 39 On vessels of the actual geometric style, for example on two of the illustrated amphorae, representations of animals are more frequent: grazing or recumbent deer, as well as various kinds of birds, lined up to make friezes that run around the vessel.

THE EARLY HUMAN IMAGE

ABOUT this time the first human pictures begin. The early picture of man is simple and essential, thought of as pure form, recreating the shape in the symbol, rather than imitating it. It is as general, and at the same time as particular, as if one were simply to say 'man.' The symbol for him is composed of geometric shapes: a hanging triangle for the broad chest, arcs of circles for the long thighs and shanks, even bands for the arms, a rectangle for the head, and on it the characteristic large nose. At first we cannot plainly distinguish whether these people are male or female. For the poet of the Iliad, the man bearing arms has outstanding validity; frankly naked in the unmistakably human figure, he is given helmet and shield, together with weapons in his hand, and they are enough to characterize him. Soon the human figure is differentiated, and man and woman are distinguished. Clothing is added, the long chiton to characterize the charioteer; the woman appears in the latticed gown, her hair falls full over her back. In the head, the powerful eye becomes important.

The many-figured representations on geometric vases are composed of such human figures. The scenes on the grave vessels have to do directly with burial and funeral rites. The wide Fig. 41 picture in the ears-zone of the great Dipylon amphora presents a prothesis, the placing on display of the dead during the lamentations. The deceased lies stretched out at full length on the high bier. The pall is spread over him – in the literal sense of 'over,' and not as it would actually appear, because it must not conceal him, since he is the essential content of the picture. Mourners, warriors among them, surround the bier, standing, sitting on stools, and kneeling. Two grown up people and a child, the next of kin, touch the pall and bier, probably as a part of the ritual. Almost all the mourners beat both arms together above their heads. To pull the hair, distort the countenance, and scatter ashes on the head and robe are gestures of mourning in Homer. The warriors grasp swords with their right hands. One of the figures sitting directly beside the bier strikes us because he extends one arm, with his fingers spread out, in front of him. He might be reciting or, as choir leader, directing the song of mourning, the *threnos*. In this picture no distinction is made between men and

41   Lament for the dead. Detail of the geometric amphora from the Dipylon (Fig. 39).

women. It may be that the small lines around the head of the figure at the head of the bier are meant to mark her as a female relative, who is pulling her hair. In the case of the deceased, whose head is surrounded by a regular series of small strokes, they may be meant to signify a wreath, the diadem of the dead. We see that with the most simple, plain signs an infinite amount of essential information can be stated.

On the great funeral crater from the Dipylon in the upper strip of pictures, the funeral procession of the dead, the *ecphora*, is represented. The bier, with its four legs, stands up above on a two-wheeled chariot, drawn by a team of two horses. The train of mourners

Fig. 42

surrounds the vehicle, taking up parts of two zones and arranged with a complete unconcern for spatial realities. Many details indicate that this representation is more recent than the previous one: there is a decided increase in differentiation and concretizing. Women and men are distinguished from one another by the drawing of breasts and genitals. The heads show the large eye. The outlines of bodies are rounder and smoother, the legs longer, the arms bent at the shoulder joints. The procession of chariots in the frieze below is probably meant to show the funeral games. In Homer, chariots and steeds circle the corpse of Patroklos three times, and after the mound has been heaped over the grave, the contests begin. Line by line, these scenes on grave vessels can be compared with the descriptions of Homer. Hardly ever in the history of the world did pictures and poetry stand so close to one another as then, not only in contents but, above all, in spirit.

As first prize in the funeral games for Patroklos, Achilles offered a woman and a mighty tripod. Tripods also appear elsewhere in Homer as battle prizes. They are given as prizes, not only in physical contests, but also for competing rhapsodists. Hesiod won a tripod at the funeral games for Amphidamas in Chalcis, and dedicated it to the Muses on Helicon, at the place where they 'first bestowed on him the gift of resounding song.' In Olympia, where tripods have been found in great numbers, they were similarly consecrated by the winners of contests at the place where the god had granted them victory in the arena. The picture
Fig. 43 in relief on the leg of one of these Olympian tripods shows two armed men struggling for the prize of a tripod (it is probably better to give this general and ceremonial interpretation to the picture, rather than to interpret it as Herakles' theft of the tripod of Apollo, since the picture lacks the elements of inequality and law-breaking). In the second picture, below the first, as though it were a Homeric simile for the mighty efforts of men struggling for the prize, we see two terrible lions leaping at each other, their jaws open wide, roaring. (Homer calls Achilles 'lionhearted.')
Fig. 44 The tripod was originally a simple cooking utensil, practically adapted for setting up on three feet over an open fire, with two large loops for lifting it off. That Homer meant just this sort of utensil is proved by his characterizing it more exactly as an 'eared' tripod (Iliad XXIII 264, 513). Tripods were used not only as practical equipment, but also as units of value in appraising the worth of things; for instance, the value of an object equals a certain number of tripods. This value is inherent in the thing itself and its material, and does not depend on beauty or art. Nevertheless, a great deal of industry and skill were applied to their fabrication. Hephaistos, the divine smith, prepared precious tripods for the broad halls of Olympus. They were provided with golden wheels so that 'of their own motion they might enter the assembly of the gods and again return' (Iliad XVIII 375). Recent excavations on Ithaca have confirmed the fact that, at the period of the geometric style, there actually were such tripods on wheels. This discovery is one of many external proofs that Homer's poem and late geometric pictorial art in the eighth century were contemporary.

42 Geometric funeral crater from the Dipylon with representation of funeral procession and games. Clay. 123 cm. high.

43 Leg of a geometric tripod. Bronze. 46.7 cm. high.

Frequently the loops of these tripods have small bronze figures as plastic decoration. This was the Fig. 45, 46 original use of the bronze statuettes of a warrior, who once held a lance in his right hand, and a horse, which were recently found in Olympia. Both figures were riveted to the upper edge of the loop and probably formed a single group, a lord leading his steed by the reins. From the middle of the eighth century on, the simple and symbolical human figure of the geometric style is also found in plastic art. What can be expressed in completely pure form in the flat painted picture has to be made more concrete in the plastic figure. But physical mass, which acts sluggishly and sinks into itself, had no importance in the human image as shown in this small plastic art. The figure as a whole, and the trunk in particular, are very flat and are pure ideas rather than natural representation. Man expresses his nature more fully in his limbs, through which he acts, than in his trunk. The long legs show swiftness; the shoulder joints and arms, dexterity and striking power; the powerful neck strength and flexibility. The chin and nose are emphasized because they express the personality. The poetry of Homer confirms this image of the human figure. He always speaks of limbs rather than the body, because in Homer 'the limbs are the lively part that strikes the eye. Strictly speaking, in Homer there are not even words for arm and leg, but only for hand, forearm, upper arm, foot, calf, and thigh. Likewise a comprehensive word for the trunk is lacking.'[11] Just as the Greek word is composed of separate letters, in utmost contrast to the Chinese ideogram, so too the Greek picture of the human being, from the beginning on, is divided up into its simplest functional parts.

Two statuettes, somewhat more recent than the Fig. 47–50 horse and his leader, dating from in the seventh century, preserve the same basic form. They probably carried a shield on the left arm, a spear in the right hand. A broad girdle, which divides the figure markedly, indicates clothing; it is limited to this symbol, because the pure naked figure is more important. In comparison to the horse-leader, these two bronze statuettes have fuller plastic rounding and more flexibility. Details, such as the waved hair, the thorax, and the wrists, are more carefully denoted. Eyes, nose, and mouth express a life force sure of its direction. The erect standing position of these small but genuine statues is especially impressive. 'Standing is the symbol of the really human, the upright, alert, and ready for action.'[12] What is expressed in these earliest of Greek human images is the activity and soundness of the human being.

In the middle of the seventh century, a new step was taken in the shaping of the human image, one just as important as the change from the archaic to the severe classical. Just as the archaic order of the kouros was left behind with the Boy of Critios, so now the geometric

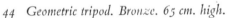

44 Geometric tripod. Bronze. 65 cm. high.

Fig. 51, 52 symbol was abandoned with the bronze statuette of a youth from Delphi. Both times it was not a matter of a sudden break, but instead, a faster unfolding of slumbering or previously unreleased tendencies. Therefore it is a simplification, and false to reality, to say that the archaic period began toward the middle of the seventh century and ended about 500 or immediately thereafter. You can no more set exact dates than you can say exactly when a boy becomes a youth, a youth a man. After some time has passed, you become aware that, in the meantime, something decisive has happened. How far the similarity between the youth's statuette from Delphi and the two geometric warrior statuettes goes can be seen at first glance; but still, the youth stands in the world in a completely different fashion. It now appears questionable whether we were justified in labeling them genuine statues a moment ago. Earthiness and the force of gravity still do not touch their essential human-ness. The Delphic youth, on the other hand, stands securely and firmly with both feet on the ground. The figure gains this greater certainty and solidity through its changed proportions. The over-slenderness of the late geometric statuettes is avoided; the size of the head and breadth of shoulders, hips, and legs are in normal proportion to the total height of the body. The arms do not move freely in the abstract space of the symbol, as do those of the late geometric warriors. We feel more strongly that they have weight; they are bent only a

*45 and 46   Geometric statuettes of warrior and horse. Decoration of the loops of a tripod.
Bronze. 15.2 and 11.2 cm. high.*

62

47 and 48   Geometric warrior statuette. Bronze. 21 cm. high.   49 and 50   Geometric warrior statuette. Bronze. 23.7 cm. high.

little, and rest evenly at the sides, with clenched hands at the upper thighs. The step-like hair is intentionally cut off above the shoulders in order that the free bearing of the neck may be seen. The shape of the face is triangular, with broad, low brow and small, pointed chin; eyes, nose, and mouth, the bearers of expression, have a more personal stamp. A broad girdle holds in the waist. As in the case of the geometric warriors, it is the only piece of clothing and is a shorthand means of expressing the whole robe; the idea of man as the pure, nude, articulated figure remains, even now, stronger than the desire for objective circumstantiality. The personal has gained greater importance; the youth of Delphi belongs to a reality that is experienced in a different manner from that of the two warriors, who are less bound to the concrete and temporal. They originate in the absolute; the youth of Delphi already stands before the world of reality, which must be experienced by him, as by everyone, in his own way. It may help us to understand this new image of the human being if we remember that Archilochos was writing at the same time, the earliest Greek lyric poet who, in contrast to the older epic poets of adventure, expressed naturally and unselfconsciously the joys, sorrows, and perplexities of a very personal 'I.'

51 and 52 *Early archaic statuette of a youth. Bronze. 19.7 cm. high.*

53 *Head of a youth from the Dipylon. Marble. 44 cm. high.*

Fig. 53

A fully awakened new human-ness, comparable to the brightness of a new dawn, is revealed in the Attic marble head of a youth found in the area of graves in front of the Dipylon at Athens, without doubt a grave statue. Of the body there remains only a clenched hand. (The statue was created by an outstanding master at the close of the seventh century.) In the presence of this head, it is hard to express in words how much solid and full-to-overflowing life is contained in the shaped marble. His eyes are brimming with a serene glance. Nothing incidental or conditional encroaches on the crystalline clarity of the form. The stereometry of the modeling is matched by the geometry of the dividing lines, the simple curving arc of brow and nose, the lens shape of the eye opening, the scroll of the outer ear, and the concentric circles of the ear lobes. In the hair, falling like strings of pearls, the separate beads are similar, but by no means identical, and they increase in size, bringing a completely objective tension. Because of the clarity and definiteness of all the shapes, the whole is a shining and alert being. His breed marks the beginning of the series of archaic kouroi, whose transformation into the classical 'portrait of a youth' we have already followed.

In vase painting, too, the prevalence of geometric forms came rapidly to an end around the turn into the seventh century, and new, free means of expression and ways of looking at things became established during the first half of that century. In this case too, it was not a definite break, but instead, a gradual transition. The tall, slender hydria from Analatos in Attica still shows many late geometric traits, such as the elongated body of the vessel with broad, long neck, plastic additions to the lip, shoulder, ears and handle, the series of oblique interlaced strokes, and the animal frieze of grazing deer and strutting birds. The scene pictured on the neck fits in with late geometric theme cycles: a ceremonial row of youths and maidens, holding hands and carrying branches, probably blossoms, between them. The bodies of the youths are shaped as though the artist had translated the late geometric warrior statuettes into two-dimensional pictures. Maidens approach the procession of youths from the opposite side. This symmetrical motion toward the center, which is occupied by the figure of a phorminx-player, provides unity of composition and content for the picture. The heraldic group of lions seen from the front view of the vessel's belly is also not new, neither the presence of lions nor their arrangement. In geometric pictures, also on vases and on gold diadems, the lions, like Homeric similes, have a deep significance: there is a man in the center, being torn to pieces by them and thus they are a powerful symbol of human mortality. Such similes now appear to suffer somewhat from the exaggerated generality of their statement. Shortly we will see, on the Chigi jug, a picture which narrates an actual occurrence. A lion bites a man in the back of the neck, a casualty of the hunt. In the meantime, the dangerous beast of prey is overpowered by hunters hastening to the rescue. What man accomplishes by himself, and how he becomes lord over the violent forces of nature, are more important than the idea that he is a slave to them.

On the Analatos hydria, the patterns are completely freed from the strictly linear patterns of the geometric treasury of shapes, and this is its striking novelty. The ornamental motifs

54 *Early Attic hydria from Analatos. Clay. 53 cm. high.*

become more like pictures of living plants. The designs under the ears and in the rear section of the main frieze look like succulent leaves and flowering shrubs. Nevertheless, it is better to think of this development from the geometric in this way: that the painter has concretized the absolute forms of the geometric style, rather than imitated and stylized natural forms. He makes his forms in nature's own way, and in doing so, displays more natural force than all the naturalists. In nature, too, the first unfolding leaves of many plants look much more abstract than the final, fully developed growth. The painter of this rejuvenating epoch no longer depends on compass and ruler, but draws his figures free hand. In general, the pictorial work becomes freer in form and ornamentation, the solid compression of objects is loosened, and soon the ornaments filling in the space between the figures will vanish entirely.

PICTURES OF LEGENDS AND GODS

If now we want to observe how, and to what extent, reality, envisioned mythically and experienced in time, is expressed pictorially in the archaic period, it is best to start once again, for the sake of coherence, with the late geometric period, the century of Homer. Mourning rites and funeral games are not the only pictures that can be compared objectively with the Iliad. Even more of its spirit comes through in the mighty battle scenes on a few craters

Fig. 55 of the sort illustrated, of which, unfortunately, we possess only a few sizable fragments. In this age, which expressed itself only in a masculine fashion and which saw the essence of man in his capacity for action, the battlefield is the area in life where the company of nobles can prove their soundness, their 'virtue.' Tightly packed like the stones in a wall, 'shield pressed on shield, helm on helm, and man on man' (Iliad XVI 215), the warriors march in the geometric picture, presented in the same unadorned but meaningful way as they are described in the verses of Homer. At the same time, they are not clearly identifiable illustrations for Homer; pictures actually based on the Homeric legends do not appear until later, and unimaginative, completely faithful illustrations did not exist in Greek antiquity until its very late period, because the Greeks always had something of their own to say in their pictures, and the painter composed, as did the singer, on the basis of the myths that had been handed down. The comparison of geometric battle scenes and the descriptions in the Iliad helps to furnish mutual enlightenment and understanding, since both pictorial and poetic statements are inspired by the same spirit, and have the same inner structure. By

55 *Fragment of a geometric crater. Clay.*

studying such pictures we can free our imagination from false notions, when reading Homer, so that, for instance, we do not think of the simple dynamics of a wave of battle in a Rubens painting, when we read of the 'tumult of Ares.' The Homeric and geometric pictures of man-killing Ares are composed of independent pictures of men, separately arranged in reference to one another. The action of battle is always seen only as a duel; in this, the pictures correspond almost completely to Homer's descriptions. The crowd of the fallen on the battlefield does not form a mass; instead, each fallen man has his individual fate. He has been hurled over on his face, struck in the neck, stretched out flat, knocked sideways; the strength is drained from his limbs, but they are not 'naturalistically' cramped. For the most part, each man has been suddenly mowed down where he stood, 'even as when reapers over against each other drive their swaths through a rich man's field of wheat or barley, and thick fall the handfuls' (Iliad XI 67). In each individual case, the man was to be described even more explicitly, limb by limb and gesture by gesture. The idea of the definite behavior of an individual man is expressed directly in the picture, as in the poem, and every unimportant elaboration of the situation is eliminated. The pecking birds between the marching warriors are not an idyllic motif, but a contributing factor. They exist as a Homeric simile: the battle-cries of the swiftly assembling warriors are compared to the loud screeching of 'wild geese or cranes or long-necked swans' (Iliad II 459). The birds in the pictures make the representation of the battlefield more audible and unmistakable.

Only simple happenings of daily and ceremonial life are illustrated on the geometric vessels. It is usually on vessels other than the great amphorae and grave craters that representations of dancing, festive processions, and games have their place: cantharoi, lekythoi or jugs, skyphoi or cups. These smaller vessels did not stand on the grave, but were placed in it as a gift for the dead, especially in body-burials of the late geometric period. Like jewel cases and jewelry, these vessels and their pictures establish a connection between the dead and life. Rows of dancing men and women; with them, the singer and lyre player with the four-stringed Homeric phorminx; tumblers jumping in the air; men beating time; prize figthers with fists or spears; and among them, unexpectedly, the symbol of human mortality – two fierce lions tearing a man to pieces with their sharp teeth.

56   Battle with a centaur. Geometric bronze group. 11 cm. high.

57   Kaeneus and the centaurs. Relief. Bronze. 33 cm. long.

Along with such pictures of life and death as they come to everyone, set down, like documentary records, in simple, fixed symbols, we also find in the late geometric style scattered examples of pictures that are very close to the heroic legends. They appear both on vases and on a remarkable type of drapery pins, the Boeotian fibulae: A woman's abduction by a man, who carries her to a large, heavily manned ship, standing ready for departure, is perhaps meant to be the rape of Helen by Paris. A capsized ship, floating bottom up on a sea full of fish, with the crew fallen overboard and grasping for rescue, and only a single man riding safely on the ridge of the keel, reminds us of the shipwreck of Odysseus. There are also a horse on wheels, like the Trojan Horse, and a man fighting a lion, who might be Herakles with the Nemean lion. But we may well ask once more, as we did in connection with the two warriors fighting for a tripod, to what extent these pictures recorded in concrete form a definite legend, and to what extent the painters' general symbolic content was later given a name, in the same way that a singer will ultimately attribute everything new and amazing that he hears about or invents to a single man, such as Odysseus.

In these pictures a lively imagination captures marvelous beings and horrible monsters. A late geometric bronze group shows a centaur and a man in hand-to-hand combat, probably a hero in the general sense, although mythology would allow us to interpret him as Herakles, the subduer of centaurs. On the other hand, a more recent representation of

Fig. 56

Fig. 57

58   Goddess of the animals. Boeotian amphora (detail). Clay. Height of the amphora, 86 cm.

centaurs on a bronze relief from Olympia, which originated after the middle of the seventh
century, in the early archaic period, can be interpreted without ambiguity. Two centaurs ram
a fully armed man into the ground with uprooted trees while, with two swords, he strikes
both centaurs at the same time in the groin, so powerfully that the sword points protrude
from the other side, and blood spurts forth. It is the legend of the death of Kaeneus, the
Lapithan, who was invulnerable, and whom the centaurs could conquer only by stamping
him into the earth. Here, as well as in the bronze group, the centaurs are presented in an
ancient form, being complete men in the front, with a horse's hindquarters attached behind.
Later the animal nature gains more ascendance in them, and they are represented with a
complete horse's body except that, in place of the neck, the upper body of a man is attached.

Exciting pictures of monsters and horrors increase in the course of the seventh century
and become frightening symbols to ward off evil. Making an image of the frightful took
away its power to frighten. Mighty griffins, creatures of an uncanny imagination, rear their
sinuous necks on the shoulders of tripods and fling open their fierce beaks. The horrible head
of a Gorgon, encircled by snakes, gnashing her pointed fangs, her broad tongue hanging
far out of her gigantic mouth, appears as a sign to ward off evil on metopes, on the gable-
ends of the oldest temples, such as the one on Corfu. Athena carries it on her aegis, just in

Fig. 60

Fig. 131

72

front of her breast, and warriors fasten it, in the shape of a bronze ornament, to their shields, to inspire terror in their opponents. Symbols of terror and power increase in this century; we can tell from the shield signs what they were: lions, the skulls of bulls, winged horses, centaurs, flying birds or crossed bones, as tokens of courage, strength, endurance, agility and swiftness. The Greek imagination was simply inexhaustible in regarding the uncanny and amazing as real, and picturing it. 'Everything that our imagination shows us,' says Cervantes, 'is so plain that we cannot distinguish it from actual experience.'

The narrative pictures of vase paintings make strikingly comprehensible the difference between archaic representations of the human being and those of the previous geometric style. The earlier pictures showed the extraordinary and ceremonial activities of the universal man. The new ones record legends, as astonishing novelties; they continue to make

59 *Entry of Apollo into Delos.*
   Melian amphora (detail).
   Clay. Height of the amphora, 92 cm.

73

the general more and more concrete, to differentiate persons more clearly, to give greater scope for experience and imagination. Men, heroes, and monsters are identified by name: Menelaos, Herakles, or Nessos. Might it be that the individuality of the legendary or divine person first begins when a name is given to him in a picture? The evolution from the general to the specific can be traced just as clearly here, in the human image, as it could in ornamentation. Following the abstract patterns which were first used almost exclusively to decorate vases, the figure-paintings of the late geometric style indicate a fruitful transition to what we consider the characteristic Greek representation of men, even though the first steps are limited to a general, undifferentiated symbolism. From the middle of the eighth to the middle of the seventh century, the transformation into the concrete legend-picture undoubtedly took place. Famous deeds of heroes and renowned adventures are unambiguously portrayed: Bellerophon on Pegasus, fighting the Chimaera; the companions of Odysseus tied under rams to escape the cave of Polyphemos; Peleus entrusting the education of the boy Achilles to the centaur Chiron. Instead of the undifferentiated generalities of actual life, the singular adventures of an outstanding individual were described and extolled in these early archaic pictures. Because of the context of mythological reality in which he appears, the human image gains an individual outline and a strong independence. Again it is appropriate to think of the contemporary lyric poet, Archilochos, who was singer, warrior and adventurer all at the same time, with the 'will to self-assertion' serving as an effective focus for his broad field of activity. To prove himself boldly and to intervene courageously in the unalterable rhythmic succession of fortune and misfortune – this applied to the early archaic vase painter in almost the same way as it did to the poet. It was the most urgent concern of the painters, and they expressed it in their pictures in the same unadorned, life-like, and penetrating way as the poet did in his verses. These early archaic legend-pictures were viable seeds sown on fertile ground, from which was reaped, in the sixth century, a magnificent harvest of narrative pictures.

It strikes us that representations of gods cannot be definitely proved to exist in pictures of the geometric period, when compared to Homer's poetry, or at least only infrequently. One of these rarities is the picture on a Boeotian amphora from the period around 700. The being who is placed, with ceremonial severity, in the center of the picture, facing straight front and absolutely symmetrical in shape, proves to be the divine mistress of animals, a divinity who has her origin in the pre-Grecian period and, after various transformations, finally ended as the Greek goddess Artemis. In this geometric picture the natural force of the wilderness is still expressed absolutely. It is quite characteristic that the lions, which appear so frequently as deathbringers to man, cannot touch this goddess with their dangerous jaws. Thus the might of the immortal is expressed visibly.

About half a century later, the all-powerful goddess of animals is shown in transformed shape on a Rhodian plate; her body is more human, but her head has become more fear-

Fig. 58

60 Head of a griffin. Caldron ornament. Bronze. 27.8 cm. high.

inspiring. She has a Gorgon face, with wild animal-mouth, and she has sprouted two pairs of great wings. What surrounded her symbolically in the older picture has now been incorporated into her body. She no longer stands in the midst of the wilderness; now she *is* the essence of the wilderness. In the more recent picture, she is not an idol, as she was in the older, but a violently intervening, pouncing, fear-inspiring, acting divinity. By the time she is pictured at the height of the archaic period, her figure has become decidedly more   Fig. 71 human, with a woman's head instead of a demon-mask.

From the middle of the seventh century, the Olympian gods of Homer were represented as human figures seen larger than life. To Naxian and Melian vase painters we owe the earliest pictures of this sort, and they achieve the same monumentality as the large plastic works that thrived at the same time. Apollo makes a ceremonial entrance into the island of   Fig. 59 Delos, which is sacred to him; four winged steeds pull his cart, on which the god appears playing a lyre and accompanied by two Muses, glorious figures with strongly expressive heads. Figures such as these allow us to surmise how the Greeks, in this early period, fashioned images of the lofty Olympian gods for cult-worship. We arrive at the actual observation of such a cult-image through a very important find in Olympia, a colossal limestone   Fig. 62 head which was fashioned soon after 600. The high crown on the hair proves that the image represents a goddess. The place of the find and its size indicate the ancient temple of Hera, where a corresponding base for a cult-image has been identified. Thus we are dealing with a cult-image of Hera in Olympia, and from the description of Pausanias we learn that it was a seated statue, and that a helmeted Zeus stood at the side of his enthroned consort. Nothing remains of this idol except the magnificent head and a fragment of relief; so it is to be assumed that only the head, or at most the hands and feet as well, was sculptured in stone, while the body consisted of a gigantic core of wood, actually clothed in a precious robe, the solemn consecration of which is mentioned in tradition. Such actual investiture of cult-images was an ancient custom, retained throughout many centuries, and it is still testified to in the classical period by the consecration of Athena's peplos on the Acropolis of Athens. This custom with cult-images of Dionysos is clearly indicated in vase paintings. Dionysos, god of vineyards and wine, of drunkenness and ecstasy, was by descent an ancient tree-god; therefore the bearded face, the mask, of the god was attached to trees, and occasionally also to poles and pillars, and the tree-trunk or post was dressed in a long, richly draped hanging. These image-pillars represented the full reality of the god, just as, earlier, he was probably worshiped directly in a sacred tree. Maenads, the attendants of Dionysos, danced around the god in this shape just as enthusiastically as though he were present among them in human shape, alive as they; sacrifices were brought to him, which is only the case with cult-images. The reliability of these vase paintings is confirmed by isolated finds of marble masks of Dionysos, one of which is plainly prepared to be joined to the wood. Masks of   Fig. 61 Dionysos sometimes appear as the predominant figure on black-figure amphorae.

Just as Dionysos, in these images, still retained much of his pre-human aspect as the god of trees and vegetation, so too the earliest cult-images of the Greeks, the Xoana, must be

61 *Neck amphora with mask of Dionysos. Clay. 39 cm. high.*   77

imagined as shapeless idols. They have been lost to us, but we know a number of things about them. On Samos, for example, a remarkable piece of wood floated to land in early times. It was found in a swampy thicket entwined with branches of the willow-like lygot shrub, and people believed that in it they possessed an image of the virgin goddess Hera. Cult-images of the earliest period, in which the godhead is believed to be miraculously present, must always be accounted for in some such fashion: they were not made by human hands, but fell from heaven; or the master who created them had a miraculous opportunity to see the god face to face in the other world. The cult of Hera on Samos became the most famous in Greece. The rites that devotees engaged in with their primitive image of Hera, rites that were not uncommon, lead us to surmise that the image of the god was regarded as an absolute reality in older times. The Xoanon was bathed during the yearly festival of the goddess, and was provided with new clothes. As we have already said, the consecration of clothing and investiture of gods are known in a number of cases. Homer testifies to the age of this custom. Although we learn little from him otherwise about the god-cults, he does tell of the pilgrimage of Hector's mother to the temple of Pallas Athena on the citadel of Troy, and how the goddess was presented with a precious peplos. It says literally that the peplos was laid on her knees; but there is still the question as to whether the words do not mean that it was placed around 'her limbs,' which in Homer's language means around her body.

Our knowledge of Greek cult-images is deplorably small. We know with certainty only one group before the Hera of Olympia: Apollo between Artemis and Leto, statues from Dreros which originated about the middle of the seventh century. They have a unique importance as cult-images, but are trifling as works of art when compared to many of their contemporaries. Sometimes cult-images are recognizable in vase paintings from the context. Even in the classic period, they are represented in an old, unmistakably archaic fashion, severely rectangular, the feet close together, the body strictly perpendicular, the head facing exactly front, and are supplied with characteristic symbols, such as a helmet and lance for Fig. 65 Athena. A colossal head of Great Greece and an enthroned goddess from Tarentum, both of which can be dated not too early in the fifth century, bear witness to the fact that cult-images adhered to the time-honored ancient form at a time when the change to a freer early classicism had already been accomplished in the statues of youths. Pure frontality, bilateral symmetry, self-confidence expressed in a smile – all are plainly features that have been carried over from old, venerated times. Phidias, in his Zeus of Olympia and his Athena Parthenos, probably created the last, and most famous, of the genuine cult-images, statues with a freshly seen spirituality which made them peers of the old. What we learn of the statue that Praxiteles created for the temple in Knidos is not enough to convince us that it was also a genuine cult-image. The first nude Aphrodite, known to us from copies, was set up in the temple with doors behind, in such a way that her beauty could be admired from all sides. But admiration and worship are completely different attitudes. The pious folk undoubtedly preferred the old images, several of which were preserved through the

62   Hera. Head of a cult-image. Limestone. 52 cm. high.

63 and 64   Menelaos and Aphrodite. Helen before the cult-image of Athena. Oinochoe. Clay. 24 cm. high.

centuries and were still highly honored in later times, because the god actually existed in them, unbeautified by the charms of art. The head of Hera in Olympia gives us the most exalted conception of these old images.

Fig. 63, 64   In the picture on a wine jug at the end of the third quarter of the fifth century, we think we recognize a turning-point in the position of the cult-image at the height of the classical period. In Troy which has just been conquered, the furious Menelaos pursues unfaithful Helen with murderous intent, and she, imploring help, takes refuge with the cult-image of Athena. Between the agitated husband and wife steps Aphrodite, in her divine inaccessibility, placing herself in front of Helen and sending out Eros against Menelaos so that, in his confusion, the bright sword falls away from his hand. This is a great dramatic scene, ranking with the contemporary tragedies of Euripides, and it has in common with them the representation of inner conflicts. In the figure of Menelaos, two conflicting impulses – stormy running and violent stopping – frustrate one another; and in this way the picture indicates the violent change of passions brought about by Aphrodite. What interests us more at the moment is the contrasting appearances of the goddesses, the distinction which

65   Goddess. Head of a cult-image. Marble. 83 cm. high.

66 *Military expedition. Chigi jug (detail). Clay. Height of the jug, 26 cm.*

the painter shows between the stiff cult-image of the armed Athena and the living reality of Aphrodite. The picture takes into account various levels of divine reality, and almost seems to express a tragic irony in showing how the old cult-image, from whom Helen piously seeks aid, remains unmoving, while another goddess surprisingly intervenes with actual help. Has a new idea of the divine here split off from the old, which found expression in the ancient cult-images, and does Aphrodite, who inspires the longing for love, now count among the goddesses as more alive and belief-inspiring than Athena, the protrectress of the city, because Athena exists in the far-distant past as a divine power, while Aphrodite is experienced in the present as a real, acting, divine force? But this thought leads us far from the point we have reached in our observations, and we must return.

THE PROTO-Corinthian vase painters, who were active in the seventh century, pictured not only hero legends but also the gay world of actual, but not every-day, experiences. The Chigi jug, with its precious pictures of the life of the nobility, is the classic example of this Fig. 66 in the third quarter of the century. It shows a military expedition, riding in chariots and on horseback, and the pleasures and dangers of the hunt. The drawing is filled with a close observation of nature; characteristic details are emphasized withouth pettiness. An advanced incision technique, cleverly used for the inner markings, allows the painter to accomplish this. In closed phalanx, the heavily armed warriors with their great round shields march powerfully along; the last ones have to run to keep up. A boy in their midst playing an aulos blares the marching rhythm into the air. The riders are busied in various ways with the reins of their long-maned steeds. The picture of the hare-hunt in the narrow band at the base has overflowing vitality; the dogs following the scent can hardly be held back, the

67 Corinthian column crater.
Clay. 44.5 cm. high.

slain game hangs in the hunter's back, and a thick bush symbolizes the abundant hunting grounds. On the opposite side in the central band we find the lion hunt mentioned earlier (cf. page 66). Experienced reality and creative condensation are here combined closely and naturally, making a charming example of Schiller's concept of the 'naïve': 'that nature triumphs as an inner necessity over art.'

Fig. 67 More 'art,' if you will, is called forth during the height of the archaic period, in the first half of the sixth century. The continuing eminence of Corinthian vase painting justifies our use of a Corinthian column crater to make the transition into the new century. The distribution of the pictorial friezes on the body of the vessel is so beautifully arranged as to seem inevitable. A broad ring encircles the wall just where the vessel's body attains its widest circumference. The main picture is worked out above this ring, and is crowned, just at the neck of the vase, with a consummate ornamental band. A frieze of riders serves as a base for the main picture; it is the same depth as the decorative bands beneath it, and together they equal the height of the main picture, bringing an impression of calm and balance in the vessel's body. The solemnity of the royal banquet, at which Herakles is a guest, demands the formal arrangement of couches and tables; they form the compositional framework on which the figures can be distributed and grouped rhythmically. Iole, the beautiful daughter of Eurytos, is fitted into the picture with wonderful thoughtfulness and meaning. The Corinthian painter's naïve joy in nature finds a delightful outlet in the richly varied characterizations of the dogs under the tables.

Fig. 68 Time-honored funeral rites and lamentation for the dead are united with a new legend-picture in the monumental painting on a somewhat more recent Corinthian hydria. The dead Achilles lies in state on the couch. His mother's sisters, the Nereids, each inscribed with her own name, lament the incomparable son of Thetis. They embrace and caress the dead man and pull their hair; one holds a lyre, to accompany the song of mourning. In contrast to the geometric representation (cf. Fig. 41) with its inevitable regularity of gestures, here hardly one is the same as another. Indeed, we could scarcely have a clearer illustration of how greatly the individuality of the person has increased in importance over a period of almost two hundred years. Here too the solemn ceremonial atmosphere prevails, and inessential details are suppressed; but in the essential thing, the gestures of the lament for the dead, there is a touching polyphony of individual expression, in which the separate strains are woven together into a resounding chorus.

Fig. 69, 70 Beside these great figure paintings on the Corinthian vases at the height of the archaic period, the animal and plant motifs that were used at the end of the seventh century to obtain a gay, tapestry-like effect in vessel ornamentation lose in importance. For a long time the Greek colonies in lower Italy and Sicily imported such proto-Corinthian and Corinthian vessels in enormous quantity: lekythoi, alabastra, aryballoi, jugs, cups, and covered pyxis, some of them with plastic heads of people and animals used for mouths and handles, are especially abundant among them. The predominating decorative motifs are animals and fabulous creatures, usually arranged in friezes, with the spaces between them filled com-

68 Corinthian hydria with lament of the Nereids for Achilles. Clay. 45 cm. high.

pactly with scatter-patterns. These Corinthian ceramics are distinguished by a strong, colorful gaiety.

About contemporary with the large figure-painted vessels of the Corinthian workshops is an Attic masterpiece at the height of archaic vase painting, the François vase, which would Fig. 71, 72 more appropriately be called the Klitias crater, after the name of the painter and the shape of the vessel. The painter covered the vessel's walls over and over, in epic breadth, with pictures. Five friezes run around the neck and belly, a sixth around the foot, and separate pictures are found on the broad sides of the great volute handles. The ornamental has had to give way almost completely before the inexhaustible eagerness for description. The apportionment of the friezes is determined by the structure and articulation of the vessel's body, and because this is so clear and balanced, the friezes are graduated in depth. The shoulder of the wide body is the culmination of the whole: there the volute handles begin, and there is found the main frieze, with its representation of a festival of the gods. The strong and integral pictorial conception here has such ascendancy that it refuses to be disturbed by the addition of the handles, and acts as though they did not exist. As though by chance, they seem to conceal parts of the procession; two pairs of gods, standing on chariots, are simply lost because of the addition of the handles, but still the painter has written in their names as he did for all the other gods: Poseidon and Amphitrite, Ares and Aphrodite. The gods in festive procession are gathering for the wedding of Peleus and Thetis. Their goal, purposely placed near the attachment of one handle, is a Doric building, through the doorway of which the enthroned Thetis can be seen, like a divine image in a temple. Peleus stands between temple and altar, to greet the gods, who are arriving by chariot drawn by teams of four, and on foot. Here the full company of Greek gods appears, in more complete numerical force than it has ever been represented except at the Parthenon and the Pergamon altar. It is as though the gods appropriately revealed themselves in their full glory at the three peaks of Greek art, the archaic, the classic, and the Hellenistic. On the Klitias crater are all the great gods of epic poetry, the gods of Homer and Hesiod, and among them the nine Muses, whom Hesiod was the first and Klitias the second, as far as we know, to name with their fine-sounding names. To present the gods festively, in holiday idleness, appears to have been characteristic of earlier archaic painting. They are meant to be seen in their sublime aspects and under extraordinary conditions. Not until the late archaic period did the vase painters 'attribute to the gods all those things which among men are outrage and disgrace,' as their contemporary Xenophanes said of Hesiod and Homer. With this picture of the gods attending a wedding in the main frieze, a larger legend-cycle is joined to a unified life-cycle, centered around Achilles, the son of Peleus and Thetis. The second frieze, on the main side just beneath the head of the gods' procession, shows Achilles as hero in front of Troy, pursuing Troilos, the youngest son of Priam. On a separate picture, which is repeated on both volute bands, Ajax carries the body of Achilles from the battle. The chariot race above the main picture may be intended to represent the funeral games in honor of Achilles. But we cannot demand a narrow limiting of theme in the genuine epic narrative

69   Corinthian aryballos. Clay. 16.5 cm. high.
70   Corinthian toilet box. Clay. 15.4 cm. high.   87

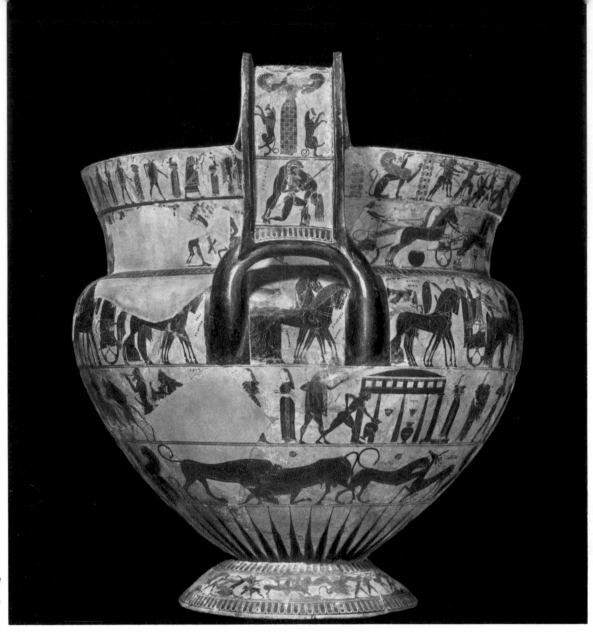

71 *Crater by Ergotimos and Klitias, so-called 'François vase.' Clay. 66 cm. high.*

and pictorial style. Among the remaining themes portrayed on the crater, Hephaistos' return to Olympus is taken from the legends of the gods, while the battle of the centaurs, the hunt of Meleager, and the freeing of the Athenian youths and maidens by Theseus are from the hero-legends. The goddess of animals shown on the handle, the battle of animals in the strip at the base, and finally the war of the pygmies on the foot complete Klitias' far-flung pictorial epic. In true epic style it embraces the exalted gods, the trials of the heroes, animals and the fearsome nature of the wilderness, and finally provides a burlesque in the battle between dwarfs and cranes, in the same way that in the fifth century, a cheerful satyr-play was added to a tragic trilogy and parodies about wars between mice and frogs were created in Hellenistic times as entertaining counterparts to the great epics. Greek intellectual life is rich in such parallels, 'mutual illuminations of the arts,' and this all-pervading unity is based on the fact that artists, especially in the early centuries, were interested in genuine statements, in 'life-like features,' in concrete realizations of legend and history, rather than in spontaneous art.

88

Not only did the painter Klitias sign this masterpiece, but also the potter Ergotimos who added to Greek ceramics a new classic type, the volute crater, inspired by metal work. It has the same basic shape as the somewhat older Corinthian long-handled crater, being distinguished only by the fact that its shoulder is not drawn in so far, that the neck with its broad lip is considerably higher, and that to the griprings have been added broad bands as handles, which rise up above the mouth and are rolled up on its edge in a scroll, or volute. The column or long-handled crater has a sturdy, full, plump plasticity, while the Attic volute crater of Ergotimos, in contrast, displays a harmonic balance between breadth and height and a freer articulation of the parts. There were a few outstanding successors to this volute crater during the archaic and severe classic periods, but they remained isolated until the height of the classic period, when suddenly there was a new, luxuriant flowering of the form, especially in the Apulian display craters of the fourth century: the vertical dimension was extended and the size enlarged almost to exorbitance, and the craters became exaggerated show-pieces for splendid artistic effects, characteristic of the end period of a culture.

73 *Neck amphora by Amasis with*
Athena and Poseidon. Clay. 33 cm. high.

It is significant that Greek ceramics of the archaic period, as they evolved from their pro-togeometric beginnings, gradually developed into several clearly differentiated classes: for example, the amphora, the jug, and the crater, which in turn are divided into certain types, the neck amphora, the body amphora, and pelice; or the foot crater, bowl crater, column crater, volute crater, kaliacrater, and bell crater. We cannot call these 'norms,' such as are known today in an age of standardization; instead, they are guiding shapes, basic patterns. The successful shape which has been gradually worked out continues to be re-worked and varied in moderation. The number of basic shapes is not unlimited, but corresponds to the practical and reasonable requirements of the family classification. In the plastic art of the period, too, we have encountered a similar basic shape, the kouros, and will learn of still others. Orderliness and clear articulation are typical throughout archaic art.

The various sections of Greece frequently showed preferences for particular families of vessels. We may note as characteristic: Corinthian lekythoi and skyphoi, Boeotian bird bowls, Melian amphorae, Rhodian jugs and plates, Laconian cups. Such classifications characteristic of a region thrived until about the middle of the sixth century. After that, inde-

74 *Lament for the dead. Fragment of a pinax by Exekias.*
Clay. Original height of the pinax, 37 cm.

pendent regional specialties yielded to the predominance of the celebrated Attic workshops, with their famous potters and painters, which reached their richest flowering during the late archaic and at the height of the classic period.

Following the generation of Klitias, there appeared, around the middle of the sixth century, two important personalities among the painters who worked with black glaze figures on a red clay ground: the Amasis Painter and Exekias. The Amasis Painter, whose modern designation comes from the name of the potter whose vessels he decorated, and who was possibly himself the potter, preferred the gods and hero legends as artistic subject matter, as did the older archaic vase painters. A neck amphora signed by the potter Amasis, which is Fig. 73 also excellent as pottery, presents on one side Dionysos and two Maenads, and on the opposite side a meeting between Athena and Poseidon. Although the gods are unmistakable because of the symbols they bear, the painter wrote their names next to them anyway, a fact that shows how much importance was attached to the name itself in early times. At ease and full of dignity, the two divine figures stand facing one another, as though holding a 'festive conversation.' The painter uses only as much of the vessel's wall – in this case, only a quarter of the circumference – as is necessary to show the monumental subject to advantage and without substantial abridgment. To the black glaze is added some red coloring for the clothing and ornamentation, as well as white for Athena's body. Incisions of masterly precision and beauty are used for the inner markings. It would be hard to find an equal to this masterpiece among the works of the same painter.

Exekias, a contemporary of the Amasis Painter, also presented divine visitations and hero legends almost exclusively, and occasionally the time-honored funeral rites: thus, always lofty and solemn themes. We can study his skill in painting and drawing in two fragments Fig. 74, 75 of clay tablets, called pinakes, which were part of the ornament of funeral monuments and, appropriately to their purpose, show pictures of funeral rites: the deceased laid out on his bier, the lamentations of the women, the funeral procession of men, and a team of mules whose shaft a servant is propping up with a stake. Here too the highest skill is shown in the perfect incisions, the incomparably delicate and graceful inner markings of the bodies and patterning of the clothes.

Exekias deserves to be known for a further masterpiece, a picture inside a cup. To decorate the circular surface in the interior of drinking bowls with figures, because of the difficulties of composition, was one of the most challenging tasks set for the Greek vase painters. They grew to meet the challenge. The pictures inside late geometric cups or bowls were encircling friezes, similar to those on the outside walls of the large vessels. These early painters were not as yet stimulated to use a single central picture; they filled the center, inside the ring of frieze, with an all-over ornamental pattern. The Corinthian vase painters were the first to develop a feeling for a central figure; at least, they found one happy solution: to encircle the central area and either fill the surface around it with ornament or leave it free, and then to fit a Gorgon's head neatly in the inner circle. We do not know whether the ancient sign to ward off evil was used for a purpose here, perhaps to startle the drinker who has surrendered precipitously to the confusions of Dionysos.

Friezes running around the interiors of cups had not yet completely fallen into disuse in the workshops of black-figure ceramic painters of the sixth century. An Attic cup of Nikosthenes, for example, displays three concentric friezes of animals and wrestlers around the framed central picture of a sphinx. A few Laconian vase painters tried in a special manner to master the limitations of form imposed by a round picture. Although it could hardly be called 'mastering' the task, one artist simply took a procession of warriors returning home, carrying their fallen comrades, and cut out a circular section in such a way that the circumference of the circle runs arbitrarily across the individual figures as though, for them the edge were not there at all. For this very reason, the picture is touching, because, in its concern for the essential, it acts so naïvely, completely unconcerned with the effectiveness of the artistic form. The reality of the representation is stronger and greater than the frame of the picture; and the frame itself is still completely independent. Not until later in the evolution of art will the two be united into a consistent whole.

Fig. 76

76 Returning warriors. Laconian cup. Clay. Diameter, 15 cm.

77 *Exekias: Sea journey of Dionysos.*
Cup. Clay. Diameter, 30.5 cm.

Another Laconian cup painter attempted the task by dividing the inside circle in the longitude of the handles into two halves, and fitting its own picture into each semicircle, in such a way that they stood head to foot. A third tried it with a radial arrangement, fitting into the circle, of four men running with long strides, their heads meeting in the center. This is the cleverest of the various attempts at solution, but still failed because the figures were not placed on a horizontal base line, which realism requires to indicate their relation to one another. The majority of the Laconian cup painters therefore ignored a radial divi-

95

sion of the circular surface and, instead, composed the picture in such a way that a line-segment formed a base for the figures and provided an unambiguous point of view. For the time being the painter does not surrender to the circular surface, but tries instead to come to terms with its limitations.

Fig. 77 Against this background, Exekias' painting of the sea journey of Dionysos inside a cup dated around 540 stands out as a remarkable accomplishment. The theme itself provided happy motifs which allowed him to fill in the field of the picture in an ingenious and unified way to the very edges of the cup. The god Dionysos sails across the wide sea, in which dolphins play around the ship. They could appear in the picture merely to characterize the sea, but they are even more closely tied to the theme; they are unfaithful mariners who threatened the god, and were transformed into dolphins as punishment. Even the grape vine is not merely an attribute of the god used to fill in the space; on the contrary, Dionysos magically caused it to grow from the mast, when he made himself known in his divine majesty to the rebellious mariners. In an informal arrangement, but composed with a con-summate feeling for artistic form, the objects fill the picture completely. Exekias' transcend-ing skill in everything he undertook is especially revealed in the way that his lively pictorial imagination included both the objects of the picture and its round shape at the same time, and combined them, seemingly without effort, into a perfect, unified whole. In this he was far beyond his contemporaries and superior to them.

At about the time of Exekias' late work, the black-figure manner of vase painting was replaced by the opposite method: that is, the red clay ground was 'reserved' from the cover-ing glaze to make the figures. In this red-figure method, incisions are no longer used and, in their place, the inner markings are executed with a fine, sensitive and flexible brush. How much more liveliness is achieved with the new method – and also, through the decades,

78 Epiktetos: Fighters. Plate. Clay. Diameter, 20 cm.

79   *Achilles and Patroklos. Cup by Sosias (detail). Clay. Diameter of the cup, 32 cm.*

how much more plasticity – is evident at once. But still, this revolutionary technical novelty meant neither a turning point nor a break in the artistic evolution. The artistic spirit's will to expression had carried forward to its utmost limits the black-figure manner of painting and drawing, and was adaptable enough to see the change of method as only a further step along the same path.

Observed as round pictures, the paintings of Epiktetos, one of the pioneers of the red-figure method, are much plainer than the Dionysos picture of Exekias. The younger Epiktetos composed his cheerful picture very simply: a nude fighter who has been proclaimed victor with a wreath, branches, and fillet, is being congratulated by a boy of about the same

Fig. 78

age, dressed in a robe. The two stand facing each other at a natural distance on a short segment of line; their heads extend almost to the upper curve. Fairly large surfaces remain free at the sides, and the painter, with a sure feeling for the gaps in his pictorial fabric, has placed his signature there. The circular form does not restrict the figures, but it also has no compelling influence on the picture. The scene might equally well be portrayed in a rectangle or entirely without a frame.

Fig. 79

It was necessary for the multi-figure picture to be fitted more forcefully into the round than is the case in this picture by Epiktetos. On a cup from the period around 500, signed by Sosias as potter, the painter discovered a more skillful way of filling the round space. He did, to be sure, use once more the segment-shaped base, from which painters before him had already freed themselves. But he composes with convincing naturalness the theme of the picture, Achilles binding the wounded arm of his companion Patroklos. From pain, Patroklos has seated himself on his great shield, forcing Achilles too to kneel down. Thus the bodies are most widely extended in the widest part of the picture's area. Achilles is bent forward naturally to pay dutiful attention to the business at hand. Patroklos has placed his legs in such a way as to give support for his elbows. Three hands are active close to the geometrical center of the circle, thus concentrating most of the movements there. The figure motif has been thought out so thoroughly and with such success that it reaches almost exactly to the edge of the space, as though the bounding circle were only a happy addition. Here the subject and the circular form have become a consistent pictorial unit, as completely as in Exekias' picture of Dionysos, but by means of concentrating the motif according to its formal possibilities, rather than by a multiplication of objects. The picture by Exekias gives an impression of carefree imagination, while that of the Sosias Painter shows extremely careful artistic effort. In this, as well as in all details of the drawing, it is characteristic of the late archaic style, to which it belongs.

Fig. 80

One of the most important masters among those who devoted their skill mainly to the painting of cups was Douris. His work begins around the turn of the century, and his late works extend into the second quarter of the fifth century; thus, in time, he stands just at the change from the archaic to the severe classic period. He conceives the Herakles theme, presented in a late work, from the genial rather than the heroic angle, as a calm picture of a state of being, rather than a description of the hero's arduous adventures. The lion's skin hangs back from his head and down over the fine chiton, and his club is laid to one side. In this way Herakles is characterized by his particular symbols, as is also Athena, the divine maiden mighty in war, by her aegis and lance. She has laid her heavy helmet aside, and the painter has intentionally placed in her left hand the owl, symbolizing her contemplative aspect. In this picture hero and goddess do not appear in their traditional guise; instead they are enjoying a relaxed fellowship quite in the manner of human beings. Herakles reaches out his kantharos, and Athena pours a drink into it from her wine jug (in which we should note the admirable rendering of perspective). The little tree, which has the artistic task of filling in the pictorial area evenly, intensifies the mood of fine cordiality, since the sinuous branching

80 *Douris: Herakles and Athena.*
Cup (detail). Clay.
Diameter of the cup, 33 cm.

of the tree's light, open crown plays back and forth between the seated hero and the modestly standing goddess, as a symbol of the dialogue at which the painter can only hint. From
the manifold names, natures, and activities which the ancients honored in Athena – the valiant
one, the efficacious, protectress of the city, wise counselor – Douris, the Athenian, chose
to profess his loyalty to the wise counselor, the tender and benevolent maiden, Pallas Athena.
Even in the Iliad she had already taken on the nature of a friend, granting advice and support
to the hero. In Douris she has completely laid aside her warlike vestments, and has been
transformed into a human being. The painter compensates for any loss in her elemental
character as a mighty and forceful goddess by giving her the refined traits of a close, friendly,
purely human existence, an image of the divine which particularly appealed to him and his
contemporaries.

While we have sought to explain the successful composition of a master of the round
picture, matters having to do with intellectual and spiritual changes have unexpectedly
forced their way into our observations about the evolution of form. When considering
pictures such as these, we cannot separate content and form, for if we did we should rob
them of what is peculiarly Greek. In them, the intellectual is given visible form, and the
sensuous has meaning. For this reason the happiest inventions of Greek painters are a sort
of poetry set down in line and form, and have made their own poetic contribution to the

81 *Euphronios: Leagros on horseback.*
    Cup (detail). Clay. Entire cup, 43 cm.

82 *Penthesilea Painter: Rider.*
    Cup (detail). Clay. Entire cup, 37.2 cm.

inexhaustible treasure house of Greek myths.

    Two cup pictures showing riders indicate the differences between the archaic and the severe classical periods, both in attitude and in expression. The older of these two master-

Fig. 81 pieces represents Leagros on horseback, and is a work of Euphronios; the more recent is from the hand of a very important anonymous painter, called the Penthesilea Painter. Euphronios' rider is a genuine round picture, in quite a different way from Epiktetos' picture of boys, although the latter is only a little older. The horse's bearing and the movement of its limbs are completely adapted to the round shape; its head is thrown back so that the curve of its chest and neck runs almost concentric to the circular edge. The legs dance in such a way that an independent base line is not necessary, and their position accompanies the circle. The division of the surface between black glaze and light clay ground is excellently balanced, and an exaggeration of the horse's trunk contributes to this effect.

Fig. 82   In the picture of a rider by the Penthesilea Painter, the round shape of the figure fitting into the circle is still more intensified. In comparison, the position of the legs of Leagros' horse appears to be too strongly determined by the circle, so that its stance is somewhat unsteady, the hoofs too close together, and the angles of the legs too sharp; and above all, the horse's trunk seems to be too heavy for the delicate legs. In this respect the Penthesilea Painter proceeds with greater naturalness and freedom, even though he never leaves the round shape out of consideration. In a wonderfully spontaneous fashion, suited to the figure, the rider's back seems to be bent and his reflective head bowed to the prescribed order of which he is a part. While in Euphronios' picture the steed and rider, in their full vigor, can scarcely

100

83 *Penthesilea Painter: Achilles kills Penthesilea.*
   Cup (detail). Clay. Entire cup, 43 cm.

84 *Penthesilea Painter: Satyr and maenad.*
   Cup (detail). Clay. Entire cup, 33.5 cm.

be restrained by the circle, the Penthesilea Painter's rider is quieter, more introspective, more collected. He is rounded off, not only by the form, but also from within. A way of experiencing life, transformed during half a century full of great events, has found its fitting expression in the human image. Leagros is a self-confident, somewhat arrogant noble, sure of his place in an organized society. The Penthesilea Painter's rider has to find his own way in a menacing world, entirely dependent upon himself and, at the same time, submitting respectfully to the gods.

The Penthesilea Painter receives his name from a picture of the killing of Penthesilea by Fig. 83 Achilles that appears inside a cup, which originated in the second quarter of the fifth century, and was approximately contemporary with the Olympia sculptures. The magnificently conceived picture fills the interior of the cup to its very edge, and seems almost to push out over it with its overflowing life. The picture is almost too much for the space, as though a subject that had been planned for the larger dimensions of mural painting had been crowded into the small space of the cup. The Penthesilea Painter's genius is especially evident in this capacity for concentration. Achilles has overpowered the queen of the Amazons in the close press of battle. Towering above her in unearthly magnitude, he plunges his sword deep into his enemy's breast. Penthesilea has fallen to her knees and, convulsively trying to ward off her destroyer, pushes against his breast and sword arm. Her death on the piercing sword is indicated in advance by two figures to the left and the right. On the right edge of the picture, behind Achilles, an Amazon lies, her limbs relaxed in death, her broken gaze resting on the ground. On the left, a warrior storms forth, casting his gaze about, eager for action. By bracketing the killing and the already killed, by alternating Greeks and Amazons, by contrasting, on the left, the warrior's sally with the queen's collapse and, on the right, Achilles' extreme display of force with the impotence of the dying Amazon, by the similarity in bearing between the figures on the right and the contrasting movements on the left, the artist has achieved a matchless contrapuntal pictorial fabric using only four figures in a narrowly confined space. But this is by no means all of the picture's mastery. The dramatic intensification of the event appears in the center, where the two royal figures rise up from a tangle of legs, only a hair's breadth apart, with Achilles' head and shoulders bent over Penthesilea; and the gazes of the two express their inner feelings with a meaningfulness never before experienced. This newness of expression and mood gives the picture its heart-rending depth. What tragic meanings of life and fate are expressed in this meeting of Achilles' and Penthesilea's gazes, we may not say, for tragedy and fate in the Greek sense have long been inexpressible.

Fig. 84   A picture inside a cup, representing a satyr who lustfully approaches a maenad, illustrates the Penthesilea Painter's remarkable talent for elastic composition in round area. The circle activates, strengthens, or compresses the motions of the two simply posed figures. The surface division into black and red is harmoniously balanced. The severely classic concept of plasticity appears in the picture; its compelling effect resides in the clear contours. The theme is old, but the archaic harshness of the natural, that phase of the antique which Mephistopheles found 'too natural,' has been taken from it. Not that these creatures of the wild have suffered any loss of natural force; it has only been (if we may use the expression) more highly spiritualized; it is present in their very essence, expands in them, and is not nature absolute, of itself. Because of the type represented by the satyr's head, and also because of the impetuous life force revealed, this picture by the Penthesilea Painter, along with his other works, is very closely related to the master of the Olympia sculptures.

After the work of the Penthesilea Painter, there was nothing new of importance to be said in round pictures on cups. From that time, they become more infrequent, and soon cease completely. Several difficult decorative tasks still remained for the art of the round picture, in metal engraving, in the making of coins, and in decorating the covers of round folding mirrors, which were popular during the fifth and fourth centuries. The round picture achieved its height in disciplined accord between content and form during the severe classical period, and subsequent developments were only in the direction of enriching and perfecting it. We may leave them out of consideration here, for to become too completely occupied with one type of picture would defeat our intention, which is simply to explain the evolution of the balanced individual picture by means of a characteristic example. The origin of the picture whose strength and artistic completeness reside in itself is a far-reaching part of the evolution of Greek art.

The inexhaustible wealth of narrative pictures in vase painting enables us to capture something of the whole bright abundance of the Greeks' world of imagination, and of their changing views. With the arrival of the red-figure manner of painting in the late archaic period, the artistic subjects of the vase painters became more varied. The sublime and heroic

85 Panaitios Painter: Theseus and Athena with Amphitrite. Cup (detail). Clay. Entire cup, 39 cm.

withdrew more and more in favor of the human and everyday. The refined society during the period of the tyrants in Athens loved relaxation, and took pleasure in an all-too-human levity, even at the expense of the gods, in their amorous adventures, their pursuit and rape of boys and maidens, and in their social gatherings, when Ganymede poured the wine for the father of the gods. Herakles rests from his strenuous adventures, and takes his ease on a couch, with food and drink. About 510 B.C. Euthymides represented Theseus, the scourge of sinister monsters and the mythical founder of Athens, as a handsome girl-chaser. In the splendid picture by an anonymous painter, he appears as a fairy-tale prince with Amphitrite on the ocean floor, to demand from her confirmation of his divine descent from Poseidon; here too Athena, with helmet, lance and owl, grants the youthful hero her advice and support. It is possible that the theme had great importance for the Athenians. The painter, however, has conceived it as a light, social affair, and executed it with the greatest elegance of form, in a manner characteristic of the latest stage of the archaic.

Carousals and erotic scenes were special favorites with the painters and their patrons. Euthymides, who placed great importance in his art and hoped to surpass Euphronios, painted a 'komos' on the body of an amphora: three intoxicated men who are frolicking and dancing wildly after a drinking party. The master's self-confidence appears to be not unjustified, when we see this picture. The spirit of Dionysos breathes out of it, the men look lascivious

86 Euphronios: Herakles wrestles with Antaios. Calyx crater (detail). Clay. Height of the crater, 46 cm.

104

87 Euthymides: Comic scene.
Amphora.
Clay. 60.5 cm. high.

105

88 Euphronios: Boys in the Palaestra. Calyx crater. Clay. 35 cm. high.

and hot-blooded, and their heavy, drunken movements are conceived largely and boldly, drawn sensuously but economically, with no pettiness. The life of music is also a welcome subject for representation. Players of citharas and aulets appear, to exercise their art in musical contests. Euphronios painted a youth with a double auloi, about to mount a podium, while daintily holding up his chiton; his audience and judges sit round about.

In the palaestra, where youths were trained, there was much for the painter to portray. Here, too, Euphronios is outstanding among the late archaic vase painters. On the wall of a kalyx-crater he unfolds a bright picture of the various preparations and physical care in a wrestling school. The boys undress, laying their robes on a stool standing ready for the purpose, pour oil into their hands from spherical flasks to anoint themselves, and one has his raised foot massaged by a small servant. The Andokides Painter, who used both the black-figure and the red-figure techniques, portrayed groups of wrestlers on an amphora, including one who is lifting his opponent powerfully from the floor, boldly shown in a front view; a foppish young Athenian is standing nearby, looking on. The Andokides Painter loved to portray such elegant youths. He shows them on a red-figure amphora as listeners at both sides of a cithara player; although, it is true, they are not noticeably attentive, and are more occupied with themselves. One of them is smelling a precious flower. In subject matter, invention, and mood, it is a lyrical picture. 'While the high poetry of the

Fig. 89

Fig. 88

Fig. 90, 91

106

epic looked toward the past and gazed at the great, the serious, and the inspiring, the age of lyricism opened men's eyes to the present, the near-at-hand, and they found significance in the everyday, the tangible, the small, and the lowly.'¹³ This observation, which was meant for late archaic poetry, characterizes just as pertinently the vase painting of the same period.

But the exalted, serious themes of mythology and the hero saga still continued to inspire important creations by the great painters at the turn from the archaic to the classic period, although now they appeared to be more concerned with their personal conceptions of the event and their manner of telling it, rather than with the event itself. For this reason, it is now permissible for us to show a representative detail instead of the whole larger pictorial context. On a second calyx crater, Euphronios pictured Herakles wrestling with the gigantic   Fig. 86 son of Mother Earth, Antaios. Euphronios' purpose is not to inform, but to design. He wants to represent visually the life forces that come into play in the adventure, to render the event clearly, very close at hand, to draw the tense play of muscles in the bodies. We would probably not be unjustified in ascribing to this master the same significance in Greek vase painting that Michelangelo has in modern art.

89   Euphronios: Youth with double auloi.
Calyx crater (detail). Clay.
Height of the crater, 46 cm.

The Brygos Painter, a generation younger than Euphronios, is no less magnificent in his presentations from the old Homeric hero saga. He decorated the outer wall of a drinking bowl, signed by the potter Brygos, with scenes from the destruction of Troy: the Greeks rage through Troy, the last Trojans fall, their women desperately defend themselves, or try to flee, like the boys. The old king, Priam, has fled to the altar in the sanctuary of Apollo, but to no avail, for Neoptolemos is already pressing upon him, cruelly swinging the corpse of the boy Astyanax. From the dying city, Akamas drags away Priam's youngest daughter, Polyxena, as a blood sacrifice. He strides along with giant steps, while the troubled virgin takes a small step and turns her gaze back once more to her helpless father. This single group encompasses the tragedy and mood of the whole.

Fig. 93

The same painter presents an important scene from the last book of the Iliad on the wall of a skyphos. Achilles has laid aside his heavy armor and rests at dinner on a couch, leaning against the cushions, in his hand one of the long pieces of meat which are hanging in abundance from the elegant table. Under the couch lies the naked, dishonored corpse of his great enemy, Hector. In the meantime the white-haired king, Priam, approaches, leaning on his staff, followed by servants bearing rich gifts as ransom for his fallen son. Achilles has turned away, and looks toward the boy with a pitcher who is standing at the head of the couch. The magnificent and gripping conclusion to Homer's Iliad is here incorporated in a

Fig. 94

90 and 91   Youth and maiden listening to a cithara player.
Amphora by Andokides (details).
Clay. Height of the amphora with cover, 67 cm.

picture, with the best means at the painter's command. But instead of simply illustrating the scene, he makes use of the individual power of expression which differentiates painting from poetry. It is impossible for the painter to represent the heart-moving, fateful, and in the end reconciling dialogue between the old man and the hero, or to reproduce the thoughtful recounting of the consequences of hospitality and mercy which brings to a close the cruel and exalted events of the poem. On the other hand, the painter may equal the poet in the meaningful expression of great sentiments. Contrary to the text of the poem, he brings together in a narrow space, in harsh proximity of place and time, the three protagonists, two living and one dead: the old man, suffering heavy sorrow, and daring the impossible; his son, once radiant and now dishonored; and Achilles, boundlessly revengeful in his pain for his fallen friend, Patroklos. In this one moment, all three hold the entire range of their natures and their bitter fate. Each one is still completely wrapped up in himself, and no relationship to the others is communicated. To the observer, on the other hand, the moment is one laden with the highest tension, like the beginning of a tragedy, when the characters of the drama are introduced. But the painter does not stop with this exposition of the characters; the continuation of the actions is implicit in the picture. It is not by chance or incidentally that Achilles has turned in the direction of the boy; he is turning away from the elderly petitioner with his gifts. The action expresses the idea that, at that moment, something is happening to Achilles, that he is experiencing a change in mood, now that his raging, his anger, and thirst for vengeance have achieved their goal. The bearing and gestures of the characters prove the greatness of the Brygos Painter. They expand the dimensions of the picture beyond the action in the foreground. This deepening of perspective corresponds to the rounder plastic art, which is also a concern of the painters of this period. The portrayal of psychological relationships, of which the Penthesilea cup (Fig. 83) provides such a significant example, is proceeding further on its way. The Brygos Painter has pushed out beyond the limits of the archaic.

In the middle of the severe classic period, at about the turn from the first to the second quarter of the fifth century, a painter pictured an event from the boyhood of Herakles on a skyphos signed by the potter Pistoxenos. Iphikles, Herakles' brother, is shown as an obedient Fig. 95, 96 student sitting opposite the old singer, Linos, who is giving him a lesson in lyre playing. The same scene is portrayed in a very similar manner on an earlier cup by Douris (Fig. 24), but the Pistoxenos Painter characterizes it more strongly, showing the old man bent and comfortable in an easy chair, and the youth sitting attentively upright, with well-bred bearing, on a stool. On the opposite side of the vessel, Herakles strides in boldly and angrily, followed by a shrivelled, white-haired nurse, pitifully limping on her stick and carrying the young lord's lyre after him. Herakles rolls his eyes threateningly. The incident was familiar to the Greeks, and they knew the fearful disaster that impended: that Herakles, averse to the Muses, would soon strike the honorable singer fatally on his head with the instrument. On his bowl, Douris portrayed Linos, in the midst of youths who are running away, sinking to the floor and seeking to ward off Herakles, who is attacking the lyre player

92   *Rhodian jug with animal frieze. Clay. 40 cm. high.*
93   *Akamas leads Priam's daughter Polyxena away as prisoner.*
     Bowl by the Brygos Painter (detail). Clay. Diameter of the bowl, 32.5 cm.

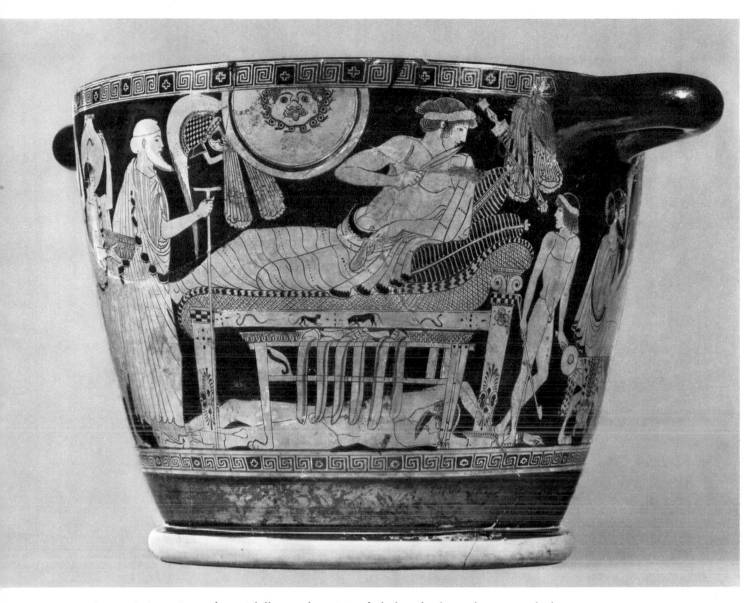

94 *Brygos Painter: Priam begs Achilles to release Hector's body. Skyphos. Clay. 25 cm. high.*

with the leg of a chair. The Pistoxenos Painter did without this full sharpening of the narration by means of action and details. He condensed the substance, in the same way that the tragedy of the period condensed the substance of the epic, and created dramatic tension by conceiving the event at the pregnant moment of quiet before the storm. The mythical event is latent, portended in the bearing of the persons who are about to act. Their basically different natures are characterized in such a way that the thing to come is tangibly established in their behavior and in the total composition. The dramatic effectiveness of the picture resides in the various strong contrasts in the fabric of the composition. The contrast begins with the contents and design of the two halves of the picture on opposite sides of the skyphos: each could be independent as far as theme and form are concerned, but still they

95　*Linos instructs the brother of Herakles. Skyphos by Pistoxenos (detail). Clay. Height of the skyphos, 15 cm.*

belong together without any doubt. On the one side, the harmonious good conduct of musical education, expressed in the balanced and unified symmetry of the two figures sitting opposite one another (here we are reminded significantly of the *paideia* even in a legendary picture as it is represented on the Douris cup); on the other side, the uncannily charged atmosphere of a coming deed of violence, made apparent in the unbalanced dynamics of the two persons walking in the same direction, all the more effective because this direction is the reverse of the usual left-to-right line of vision. Strong contrasts are also apparent in the separate halves of the picture: the relaxed old man and the taut youth on one side, the crooked old woman and inflexible Herakles on the other.

The greatness of inner vision and the talent necessary to express the old myths pictorially were granted to only a few outstanding painters. Toward the middle of the fifth century, vase painting reached an even greater crisis, when it sought to keep pace with the new techniques of large mural painting. The vase painter tried to produce a strong plastic effect in the individual figures, as mural painting did, and to make clear the graduated spatial relations of the figures to one another and to the background.

Isolated late masterpieces of Greek vase painting still ranked with the other arts, because

96 *Herakles about to slay Linos. Detail of the opposite side of the skyphos Fig. 95.*

Fig. 97

they succeeded in expressing the high classic style in their own manner. During this period it became possible to express the psychological in a way that had never been attempted before. An anonymous painter tried to represent in visible form on a crater the invisible power of music to move the spirit. To express sound and hearing by means of form, to make the invisible visible, presupposes a penetrating imagination and a rich gift for invention; this unknown painter, a great artist, had a command of both. Orpheus has arrived among the rough Thracians. The mythical singer, whose music could affect even the stern lord of the underworld and move him to give back the dead Eurydice, sits on a rock surrounded by splendidly dressed youths and men, and touches them powerfully with his singing and playing of the lyre. One of the youths stands still, leaning on his spear, with his eyes shut, totally absorbed in listening. A second is overcome with emotion to such a degree that he leans on his comrade for support. Opposite them, the next Thracian is filled with rapt attentiveness; he seeks to read the song from the lips of the enthusiastic singer. The last, the manliest of the four, seems to show little response, in his manner and bearing, to the alien rapture. Orpheus has lost himself in singing and playing, and his ecstatic gaze is raised to the heights from which his inspiration, the gift of the Muses, comes. The coherence of the figures, which seems to be based completely on something within them, is no less apparent in the way they are placed in relation to one another in the general composition. The varied relationships in the arrangement, bearing, and motion of the figures, the balance between the main motif and the subsidiary motifs, the placing of the two pairs, and the triad of the center and the sides, all give the picture such a tightly-knit unity that it needs no frame. It is a great masterpiece of classic composition; even Raphael did not surpass it, and hardly achieved the simplicity and clarity of a Greek picture such as this.

'To be economical with expression and gestures' is Goethe's recommendation to the artist who wants to produce something significant. The greatest works at the height of the classic period are unassumingly simple and self-evident. The main picture on a stamnos by the Kleophon Painter is an outstanding example of this. Designed as simple standing figures, moderately plastic, the heads completely in profile, a youthful warrior in full armor and a maiden wearing a plain, ungirdled peplos stand facing one another. In a correspondence of opposites, similar to the figures on the Penthesilea cup, an old man and a female servant follow them on each side, their positions probably reversed for the sake of art. The maiden holds a jug, from which she has poured wine, in her right hand, hanging at her side, while the warrior lifts the cup she has filled to his chin. As he does so, his gaze rests with strong

Fig. 98

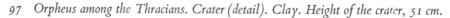

97 Orpheus among the Thracians. Crater (detail). Clay. Height of the crater, 51 cm.

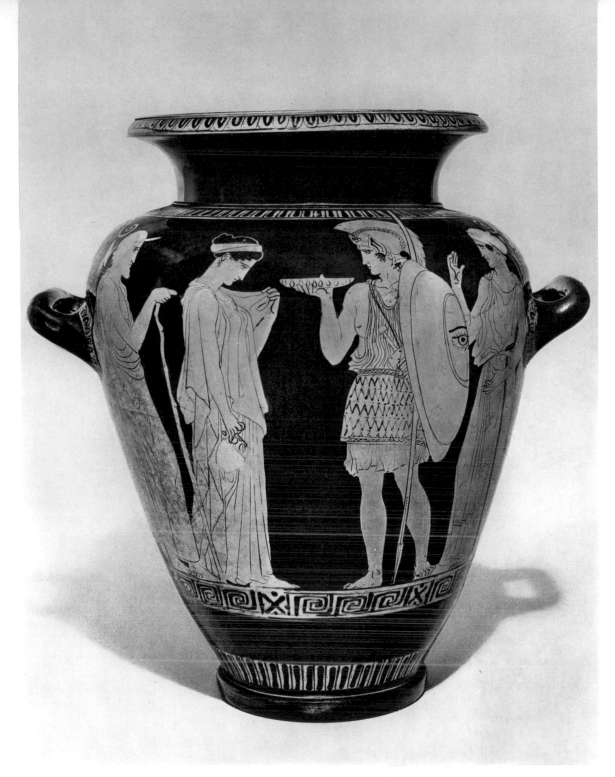

98   Kleophon Painter: A warrior's farewell. Stamnos. Clay. 44 cm. high.

manliness on the maiden, who modestly and fervently bows her head and lowers her gaze. The participation of the old man leaning on his gnarled stick, probably the warrior's father, and the female servant, whose hand is raised in a gesture of farewell, is only hinted at; and this makes all the more effective the expressiveness of the central group, where deep feeling is given visible form. The painter presents the maiden and the man as completely independent and absorbed in each other, as though self-awareness and a realization of their relationship has first come about through this encounter. The man seeks to express affection and trust through his gaze and bearing; it is only by such ambiguous phrases that we can try to describe their absolute merging in one another. The grandeur and sublimity of the pair have given rise to the surmise that they are meant to represent Iphigenie and Achilles, but it is probably better to avoid such an interpretation. These two beings are so unconditionally human that to give them names would be to limit their absoluteness. With them, the human image at the height of the classic period returns to the pure figure with which it began in the period of the geometric style. A language so simple as that used in this stamnos picture reminds us of Homer, of the farewell of Hektor and Andromache. Through manifold stages, from the Doric migration to the height of the classic period, the Greek spirit remains an unbroken unity. It is constantly concerned with what the human being is; and the answers, as revealed in pictorial expression, are self-realizations. 'Art' remains in the service of an understanding of man.

SANCTUARY AND TEMPLE

To UNDERSTAND Greek buildings and sculpture, it is really necessary to know the country of Greece: the bright, radiant light, the transparent air, the sculptural solidity and magnificently formed pattern of the barren mountains, the confined vistas of the plains, the division into separate regions, each with its own individuality. In Greece the land and sea interpenetrate one another intimately and profusely, in bays, extended promontories, and islands, so that there is no place where man can escape from the nearness of other human beings. The Greeks sought society, not the solitude of nature. 'Fields and trees have nothing to teach me,' says Socrates to Phaidros, 'but the people in the city do.' The Greeks' aesthetic spirit found appropriate expression, not in a poetry of solitude, but in the conversation and instruction of men as social beings. It reached its peak in the drama, in dialogue, and in didactic poetry. The Greeks did not paint landscapes; natural objects, such as trees, bushes and flowers, were used almost exclusively in their pictures to explain more exactly some human occurrence. Boys getting ready to swim hang their clothing in the branches of low trees; Achilles hides behind a bush in order to spy on Troilos; grapes are harvested from the vines, and olives are knocked down from olive trees. The living animal, on the other hand is a much more important natural object to the Greeks, either as a symbol of violence, or as a menacing force that is fought and destroyed by the hero, or as a useful tamed animal. Pic-

99 *Erechtheum. Acropolis, Athens. Marble.*

tures of animals are frequent in sculpture as well as in painting. The Greeks are interested in their fellow men, including the gods, and not in man's environment. So completely was everything focused on man that finally, at the height of the classic period, the sophist Protagoras, the friend of Pericles, wrote: 'Man is the measure of all things.'

Nevertheless, the visitor to Greece is constantly enraptured by the scenic aspects of the Greek sanctuaries, the second great stage that is so essential for the effectiveness of Greek buildings and statues. At the southern tip of Attica, on the bold cape of Sunion, the temple of Poseidon extends far into and high above the island-dotted sea. A splendid wreath of large mountainous islands surrounds the small, sterile, rocky island of Delos, with its famous sanctuary of Apollo and Artemis. On Aegina, remote from the harbor and the commercial city, the temple of Aphaia offers a panoramic view over the Saronian Gulf to the plains of Attica and the Acropolis of Athens. In the rugged high mountains of Arcadia, the traveller comes with surprise upon the temple of Apollo of Bassae, and is rewarded with a commanding view over Messenia to the southern sea. The sanctuary of Olympia lies in peaceful seclusion, surrounded by protecting mountain ranges, near where the Kladeos flows into the Alpheios river. In aloof splendor, the sacred oracle of Apollo of Delphi is situated high in a world of mountains.

However, the presence of a beautiful view for nature lovers did not determine the choice of these wonderful sites for Greek sanctuaries; they were decided, instead, by the gods to whom the sanctuaries are dedicated, and their miraculous appearances on earth. It is because the sublime and mighty influence of the gods can be experienced in these places that they are so magnificent and are preferred above others. Zeus, who gathers the clouds together and hurls lightning and thunder, inhabits the high mountains and, along with all the great gods, Mount Olympus. Poseidon, who rules the sea and also shakes the earth, has his sanctuaries on promontories, which are dangerous for mariners to circumnavigate, or in earthquake areas, such as the Isthmus of Corinth, where the land is hemmed in by the sea on both sides. Many sanctuaries were far removed from cities, or at the outskirts of a city. The remoteness from the city to which they belong is characteristic of most sanctuaries of Hera, such as those of Argos, Samos, Croton, and Paestum. But the protectress of a city has her temple in the center of the town, preferably on an ancient citadel. The Acropolis of Athens fulfills both requirements magnificently for Athena.

No other temple is so intimately merged into the urban community as the Christian church; in baroque times its façade even became part of a row of dwellings. The Greek temple needs space; this is true because of the nature of the building, and even more because of the nature of the religion. The Hephaisteion in Athens, to be sure, is located directly on the marketplace, like the city church in the Middle Ages; but it is still completely separated from it, rising considerably above the Agora on a steeply sloping rocky terrace. Today this temple lies completely in the open, and gives a strong impression of consistent plastic corporeity. In ancient times it was surrounded by a grove, planted and cultivated with difficulty in ditches in the rocky ground. The trees in such groves were determined by the particular

100 Athena molding a horse. Attic jug. Clay. 21.5 cm. high.

god to whom the grove belonged, in cases where a mythical relationship existed between the god and a certain plant. Oaks were sacred to Zeus in Dodona, pines to Poseidon on the Isthmus, laurel to the Apollo in Delphi, and myrtle to the Aphrodite of Knidos. The temple and grove, together called the temenos, or enclosed precinct, were separated from their surroundings by a wall. Frequently sacred roads led from a great distance to the sanctuary: from Athens to Eleusis, from Miletos to Didyma, from the harbor city of Epidauros to the Asclepieion, and from the sacred harbor of Delos to the precinct of Apollo. Mighty statues bordered these sacred roads, either separately or in long files. On the road by which cere-

Fig. 102 monial ambassadors ascended to the sanctuary of Apollo on Delos, a number of upreared lions still watch today, statues of great tenseness and plastic force, which were created in the second quarter of the sixth century from Naxian marble by the sculptors of neighboring Naxos.

Delphi probably provides the most comprehensive idea of what appertains to a Greek sanctuary. Its physical setting is the most magnificent in Greece. In mythology, its founding reaches back to the time of the gods, and its history is venerable. Through the power of its oracle, it had an important influence on political affairs and colonization, on legislation and

Fig. 101 morality, and its fame radiated far beyond Hellas. The Delphic sanctuary has a very high site, and can be reached from any direction only by intricate and difficult paths. The huge center of the mountain chain, Parnassus, which shelters it from the raw north wind, here pushes forward to the southwest in two steep, barren limestone cliffs, the Phaidriades or 'polished rocks,' at the foot of which the sanctuary lies on rising terraces, enclosed in a semicircle by them and their spurs. In front of the temple the mountain plunges down into a deep and partly inaccessible gorge. Through it the brook Pleistos makes its way, and then flows through a broad alluvial plain, thickly wooded with olive trees, to the sea. It is the Gulf of Corinth, hidden by the ridge of Kirphis for some distance, until the view opens out on the Bay of Cirrha across which, in the distance, can be seen the mountains of Locris and the Peloponnesus. It is a portion of the earth singularly characteristic of the concentrated multiformity of the Greek countryside, with its mountains, plains and sea.

On clear days, eagles draw calm circles around the peaks of the Phaidriades, on the hot slopes of which their prey, the snakes, sun themselves; and we remember the ancient tale that Zeus sent out two eagles from the opposite ends of the world, so that he could determine the center of the earth by their meeting place. They met in Delphi, and that is why a relief dedicated to Apollo shows the god in front of the earth's navel, with an eagle sitting on each side of it. At times, after days of rain and fog, it happens that a mysterious streak of mist is suddenly expelled from the deep, unscalable crevice in the rocks between the Phaidriades, as though the gorge had exhaled a poisonous vapor. It remains motionless for some time, then spreads out immensely and darkens the whole valley with a thick layer of clouds, so that the steep paths become dangerous. As suddenly as it came, it vanishes again after a few hours, drifting apart and finally absorbed by the rays of Helios. Once again Delphi lies in bright light. The sun's rays are reflected blindingly on the Phaidriades, the

101 *Delphi. Sanctuary with Temple of Apollo.*

animating warmth is caught in the funnel of the surrounding mountains, and an indescribable glory of gay spring flowers and fresh greenery unfolds on the slopes. We are reminded again of an ancient myth, buried under layers of changing traditions. The earth mother, Ge, gave birth to a monster here, the gigantic dragon Python, who occupied the whole area and dragged his uncanny coils around the mountains. The place was named Pytho after him, and continued to be called that for long time. Then Apollo arrived there on his travels from Olympus, searching for a spot suitable for his sanctuary. He killed the earth-born Python, and himself laid the foundations of his temple. Transformed into a dolphin, he led mariners who were on their way to Crete around the Peloponnesus into the Bay of Crisa, and made them priests in his sanctuary. This is the explanation of the name Delphi, which the place later bore, and Apollo, who was worshipped as Apollo Delphinos, the protector of seafarers, in Knossos, Crete, was known in Delphi as Apollo Pythios, ruler over everything primordial and lord of the oracle, which had once been the ancient prophetic voice of the earth and now issued from the mouth of his priestesses, the Pythia. The crevice over which they are supposed to have sat with their tripods and breathed in the intoxicating vapors has been sought in vain in the temple. Behind this legend may be hidden ancient memories of

123

102   *Street of Lions in Delos. Marble.*

the mighty gorge between the Phaidriades, of the primordial cult and the oracle of Ge, reduced to a small crack in the rock of the sanctuary. We must be aware of these rich, many-
layered mythological traditions, if a Greek sanctuary is not to remain mute for us, and if
we want to feel again something of the mighty life and the secret meaning of the sacred
place.

    The visitor who enters the sacred precinct of Apollo, a great rectangle enclosed by solid
walls, through the old, plain gate and climbs up to the temple itself on the sacred road is
accompanied on both sides, for a long part of the way, by votive offerings of the Greek
city states for important victories which they achieved over one another – a sad memorial to
Greek dissension and the decline of Greek freedom, although among them is one joyful
monument, the golden tripod celebrating the common victory of the Greeks over the
Persians at Plataea in 479 B.C. The memorials have been plundered and destroyed till little
more than their pedestals remained, and it requires a lively imagination to reconstruct the
wealth of votive gifts and free-standing statues that originally graced the sanctuary. Men-
tally we have to set back in their old places in the bright sunshine many splendid treasures that
are now housed in Greek museums: in Delphi, for example, the charioteer, the twin group
of Kleobis and Biton, and the Sphinx which was presented by the Naxians. This Sphinx is the
oldest of the Delphic votive offerings that has been preserved, and it once stood on a pillar

Fig. 28, 29
Fig. 16, 103

124   103   *Naxian sphinx in Delphi. Marble. 232 cm. high.*

almost ten meters high, with narrow, sharp-edged fluting and a very ancient Ionian capital, a mighty sentinel, its head raised high above its forepaws, looking straight ahead, with great, beautifully curved wings. Judging by the work, it is an older relative of the lions on the sacred road of Delos and, like them, a Naxian product from the height of the archaic period.

Fig. 104   In imagining what has been lost along the Delphi path, we might call to mind several archaic marble statues from the Acropolis in Athens, to give wider scope to our picture. The statue of a calf-bearer was erected there around 570, a stately bearded man carrying a bull calf on his shoulders. It is an image that the visitor to Greece in the Easter season frequently encounters in the form of a man carrying a lamb, the Good Shepherd of the early Christian period. The Good Shepherd, however, conceals a symbolic meaning behind his outward appearance, while the calf-bearer is nothing beyond what he actually represents – a man bringing a young calf to the goddess in her sanctuary on the Acropolis and placing himself

104   Calf-bearer from the Acropolis. Marble. 165 cm. high.

in the service of the divinity. The man's name is inscribed on the statue, Rhombos, and this makes it a definite person, although it is not the portrait of an individual. We have no further details about the donor, and can only guess that he is specially authorized to represent a community. As a human being, as well as an image, he stands in a firmly established order, at that time the government of Solon in Athens, and as a person he has his place, in accordance with Solon's somewhat older elegy, in the definite order of the ages of man. The statue is strictly frontal and bi-laterally symmetrical; the animal's legs and the man's arms grasping them make a geometrical cross on his breast. But in spite of – or perhaps because of – this constraint, the image abounds in life, because it is completely unambiguous and open, directed outward, with no trace of introspection.

Kouroi, such as we have already observed, would not have been lacking in the Delphic sanctuary; they are especially numerous in sanctuaries of Apollo. In the sanctuaries of female divinities, figures of maidens, the korai, predominate. At their head stands the oldest known life-size Greek marble statue; a landmark at the beginning of the archaic epoch, it is dated about the middle of the seventh century. Nikandre, a woman of Naxos, dedicated it to Artemis in her sanctuary on the neighboring island of Delos. We learn this from the votive inscription, in which the statue speaks in the first person. Other statues of the archaic period speak similarly in their own persons, thereby indicating to us how the early Greeks experienced such a statue as independent and existing in itself. We must understand them in

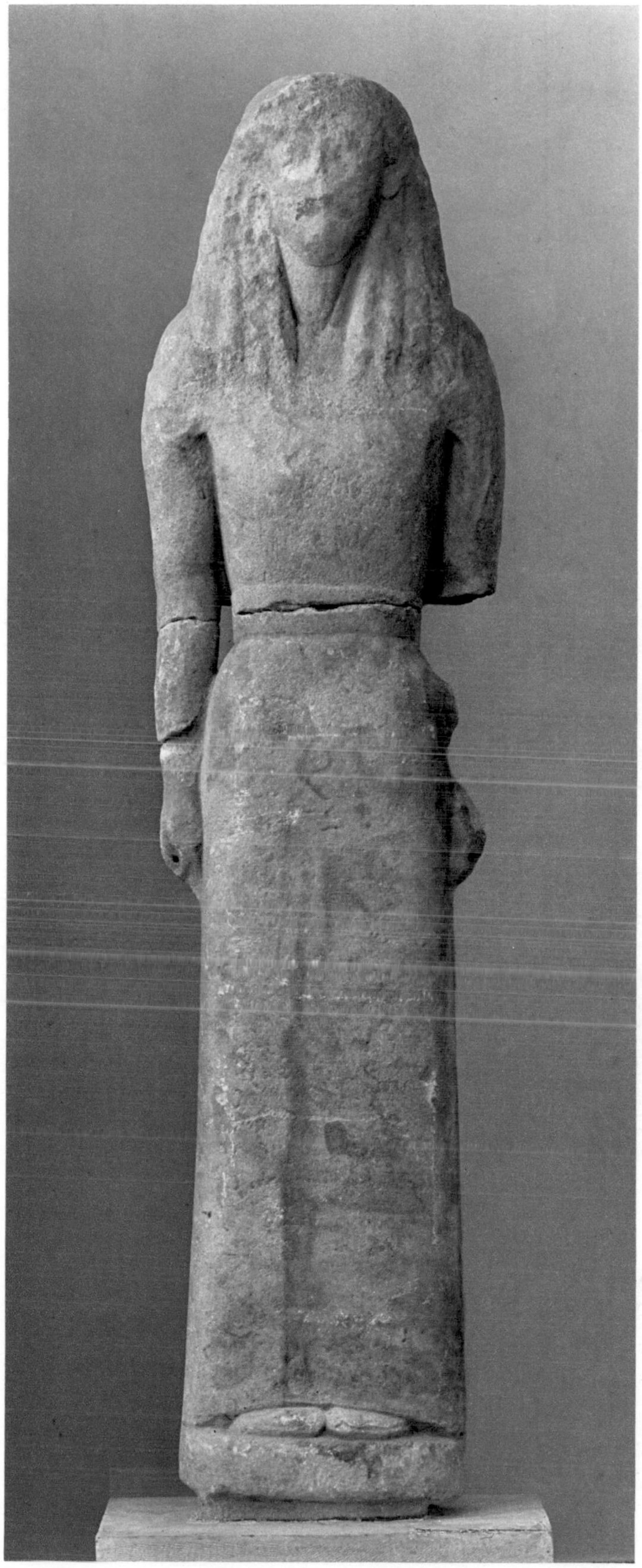

Fig. 105

105 *Nikandre from Delos. Marble. 175 cm. high.*

the same way. According to the words of the inscription, the statue must be intended as a person other than either the donor or the goddess, for it reads: 'Nikandre dedicated me to the far-aiming arrow-shooting goddess.' But, since we still comprehend almost nothing of the mysterious rites of early aboriginal cultures, it is better not to pretend to too much wisdom about the matter, and instead, to see as an important and decisive reality the objective encounter of donor and goddess in the inscription. Nikandre's statue on Delos has a time-honored simplicity of form. The human figure is developed cautiously and still positively, out of the angularity of a rather flat block of marble. She is tall and, naturally, holds herself in the archaic manner, symmetrically and facing straight ahead. The head still retains much of the geometric shape, with the face like a triangle pointing downward. The hair falls in broad masses at each side, over the shoulders; her arms lie closely at her sides, and a broad girdle divides the body.

A somewhat smaller female figure marks a significant step forward in the representation of the human image in sculpture. We do not know where it was found, and it is called the 'Woman of Auxerre' from the place where it was formerly preserved. The Woman of Auxerre differs from Nikandre's statue not only in time (she originated about a decade later), but also in region. Her features are familiar to us in Cretan works, such as the small globular jug with a plastic woman's head as the opening. Although in the Woman of Auxerre we are still clearly aware of the squareness of the limestone block from which the figure is shaped, particularly in the large surfaces of the skirt, still she is fuller, less board-like than Nikandre's statue. There is a definite increase in rounded corporeity and articula-

Fig. 107

Fig. 106

106 *Small Cretan jug with plastic head of a woman. Clay. 10 cm. high.*

107 *'Woman of Auxerre' (detail). Poros. Height of the whole figure, 65 cm.*

108 and 109   Peplos Kore from the Acropolis. Marble. 118 cm. high.

110 Kore from the Acropolis. Marble. 92 cm. high.

111 Kore from the Acropolis. Marble. 54.3 cm. high.

131

tion. The bearing of the figure is freer; only the left arm is straight, with the hand pressed flat against the skirt; the right arm is bent at a sharp angle, with the right hand laid expressively on the breast. The gesture has a definite meaning, one that is now lost to us, but probably has religious significance. Her head, too, diminishes markedly from a broad, low forehead to a narrow, but powerful chin, and a mass of regularly arranged hair falls down over her shoulders. The expression of the face, with its firm, clear drawing of eyes and mouth, is alert and enterprising. Like Nikandre's statue, the Woman of Auxerre also comes from a sanctuary. In the severe order of their forms and the ceremonial dignity of their bearing, they show that they are intended for the service of a divinity.

Athena's sanctuary on the Athenian Acropolis has yielded a great many archaic korai. These female statues were presented not only by Athenians, but also by people of other states, and for this reason provide us with a vivid picture of the varied realities of life in Fig. 108, 109 archaic Greek times. One of the earlier korai is a maiden wearing the Doric peplos. This modest woolen garment produces such a severe, squared effect that the statue seems to fit in with the two earlier female figures, although it was actually made a hundred years later. Of course, on closer observation, the more highly evolved shape of the Peplos Kore is unmistakable; but the preserved homogeneity of the kore as a type is an essential characteristic of the archaic, found also in the kouroi.

Fig. 110, 111 Most of the korai from the Acropolis were made in the last quarter of the sixth century, and wear the more pleasing Ionic costume. The supple, closely pleated chiton is not hidden so completely as it is on the Peplos Kore, because the short mantle over it covers mostly the upper part of the body. It is usually fastened on the right shoulder and at the right upper arm, and its broad border descends diagonally in front of the breast and under the left arm. This small mantle's freely falling festoon of folds of varying lengths, and the chiton, which is caught up at one side to allow greater freedom of pace, provide the sculptor with many opportunities for ornamental distinctions in the details. Many of these korai still retain today much of the original bright painting of their hair, eyes, and lips, as well as the borders Fig. 111 and patterns of their clothing. On an excellent kore of Chian marble, an eastern Greek work dated around 510, the chiton was once dark blue, and the mantle had a red border edged in blue and a blue scatter-pattern; her lips were red, and apparently her hair also, which was Fig. 112 crowned with a blue diadem patterned in red. A female terra-cotta head, found in Olympia and dated at about the same time, might be mentioned in this connection, although it does not come from a kore. The soft, luxuriant contours and her crafty expression lead us to Fig. 70 think of Ionic art. Of a completely different, and harsher, nature is the small female head that forms the handle of a Corinthian pyxis. A verse by Archilochos sets down, more fittingly than we can today, the unique essence of the early Greek concept of the maiden[14]: 'She rejoiced in the blossoming rose and / the myrtle branch in her hand. Her hair / overshadowed her shoulders softly, and her neck. / From her head and breasts the myrtle oil sent forth its fragrance. / In her presence even an old man would still have felt longing.'

112   Female head from Olympia. Terra-cotta. 14 cm. high.

Fig. 114

Fig. 113

After this glance at several votary statues, let us look around further in the sanctuary of Delphi. A mighty wall crosses the sanctuary, and before it on steps are several slender, thinly spaced Ionic columns, the remains of a hall which the Athenians dedicated to hold their booty after their victory over the Boeotians and Chalcidians in the year 506. The wall, which serves as a retaining wall for the temple terrace, presents a strange appearance. Great polygonal blocks, with even surfaces on the exposed sides, are fitted closely together, in spite of their irregular angles. The carefully hewn blocks have been very skillfully placed so that the seams where they join form a delicately notched, decorative pattern of lines over the whole surface, a series of curving movements with small branchings and counter-movements, ascending powerfully, and descending shallowly; the straight joints, for the most part perpendicular, are clearly treated as of secondary importance. This late archaic polygonally jointed wall concludes a long evolution in early Greek masonry, which can be traced back into the geometric epoch, and is characteristic of archaic polygonal masonry. In this field, as in so many others, the beginnings of the Greeks' artistic accomplishments are simple and determined by nature. They took rubble, fragments of rock from the local limestone mountains, in its original irregular, haphazard shape. The stones were carefully selected, tested, and evaluated for support, weight and thrust. Then small and medium-sized stones were firmly piled up and reinforced with clay. Relatively flat fractures with large surfaces were placed facing outward and fitted together to make an even appearance. The result was a wall 'with close-set stones, to avoid the might of the winds' (Iliad XVI 212f.), as it was described as long ago as Homer's time.

Retaining walls of the classical period abandoned polygonal masonry, and used the ashlar work, with squared, dressed stones, which reached its highest perfection at that time. In the sixth century, the evolving art of ashlar masonry had its individual, archaic features. Delos had access to an especially valuable building material in the neighboring marble islands of Paros and Naxos, and by the end of the geometric epoch had already developed

*113 Archaic polygonal masonry.
Retaining wall of the Precinct of Athena,
Delphi. Limestone.*

114　*Late archaic polygonal masonry. Retaining wall of the Temple of Apollo, Delphi. Limestone.*

a much more regular masonry than the polygonal work of the mainland, using stratified quarried stones. Since marble breaks into strata more evenly, and can be piled up more easily in continuous layers, it is understandable that ashlar work developed earlier on the islands than elsewhere. Early in the sixth century ashlar construction, with even wall surfaces and horizontal and vertical jointing, had already been mastered there. A more individual feature is the stepped-off, sharp-edged corner, which is an element of the order and Fig. 115 emphasizes the erectness of the wall. The individual blocks are still of unequal size, of unequal height in the various layers, and of unequal width in one layer; that is, the individual component parts of the ashlar wall still retained something of the original independence of detail that was natural to polygonal masonry. Uniformity and subordination to the whole were not as yet desired. This is an essential trait of the archaic, one that can be observed over and over again.

Fig. 99 The form of the ashlar wall at the height of the classic period is best seen today in the Erechtheum on the Athenian Acropolis. The classical period is so permeated with the spirit of simple order and lucid articulation that, even in the retaining wall, the whole and its component parts are designed to stand in a solid, unambiguous relationship to one another. All the blocks are of the same size, and so placed that the vertical joints of every second layer are aligned. While in polygonal masonry the intractable blocks press powerfully against one another at their irregularly placed joints, and weigh heavily upon one another, the ashlar wall counteracts this impression of conspicuous heaviness by means of a harmonious equalization of gravity and bearing force in each individual block, and by its regular system of horizontals and verticals in the wall as a whole. In polygonal masonry, an impression of strain prevails, while, on the other hand, the perfectly fitted joints of the layers and the side-surfaces in ashlar work express something effortless. When, in addition, the individual blocks are not extended, but are relatively compressed, then a greater number of vertical joints are brought into the play of forces, and this increase of supporting perpendiculars counteracts the ponderous horizontals. Each quadrangular block contains in its own proportions the mass and relationships inherent in the whole; it is more than merely a means, it is the creative potential of the wall. Never before was a wall articulated in such a way, down to its component parts, from simple forms and with absolute logic, as the classical Greek ashlar wall. It is not an imposed shape, but an intensification of its very substance. The wall is completely what it appears to be, and nothing else, for the blocks go all the way through; it is not a showy veneer applied to a core of an entirely different sort. The stone-

115 Archaic ashlar. Letoon, Delos. Marble.   *116 Retaining wall at the height of the Hellenistic period. Hellenistic Hall, Delos. Marble.*

136

117   Treasury of the Athenians, Delphi. Marble.

work of each individual block is extraordinarily exact, neat, and workmanlike. All in all, the ashlar wall is so right in material, so right in workmanship, so replete with meaning and art, that it would be hard to imagine how anything could be more classical.

A brief glance at a retaining wall on Delos from the height of the Hellenistic period, at the end of the third century, may serve to confirm our assertion at the beginning of this book about the prevalence of 'art' in Hellenism. What this wall displays is no longer naïve polygonal masonry; here the artist intentionally introduces the irregular and odd. Continuous horizontal joints are largely retained, but they are occasionally interrupted by a big block shoved in unexpectedly, to counteract the monotony. In the side joints the greatest variation prevails, in a completely successful attempt to make the wall charming. The whole shows an exaggeration and disregard of proportions which the classic builder would have dismissed as arbitrary, and a trifling with the practical purpose which the archaic builder achieved painstakingly through the laws inherent in the material.

Fig. 116

137

118   Temple of Poseidon, Paestum; from southwest. Limestone.

Fig. 117

Various kinds of treasuries once distinguished the sanctuary at Delphi. Today only the reconstructed treasury of the Athenians can be seen in its entirety. Like almost all known treasuries, this is a small building of the type known as distyle *in-antis*: closed walls on three sides, two supports on the entrance side between the antae (free ends of the side walls), and a short porch (pronaos) leading to a simple inner room (cella). In the Athenian treasury the two columns between the antae and the entablature are Doric, and the metopes around the building are provided with figures sculptured in relief. A ridge roof covers the building and gives rise to the broad triangles of the gables (pediments) over the two narrow sides. Other treasuries, the most important among them the one which the islanders of Siphnos established around 525 B.C., use the figures of two maidens as supports, bearing the entab-

Fig. 137–142

lature by means of baskets on their heads. In this case there is no triglyph frieze above the architrave, but instead a continuous frieze, which in the Siphnian treasury is decorated with scenic reliefs. Two treasuries, one of them established by Massilia, the ancient Marseilles, have *in-antis* columns with peculiar calix capitals – not an imitation of plant motifs, as the name would suggest, but a free invention, a series of vertical grooves which open out and round over at the top, not unlike an egg-and-tongue molding.

In the center of the sacred precinct at Delphi stood the Temple of Apollo. Today little more of it is visible than the foundation. If we want to make the acquaintance of a Doric

119 Temple of Poseidon, Paestum; east side. Limestone.

Fig. 118, 119

temple, it is best to turn to Paestum, where the so-called Temple of Poseidon has remained quite complete — or at least more complete than any other Greek temple. The peripteral temple, with its colonnades, the peristyle, surrounding a rectangular cella on all sides, was not only, as a religious edifice, the most important task of the Greek architects, but also, as an architectural creation, the most supreme accomplishment of Greek art. In comparison to the equally magnificent architectural masterworks of other great cultures, whether Egyptian mausoleums or Gothic cathedrals, it is distinguished by its simplicity, consistency, and self-sufficiency. It is unusually corporeal, not only by virtue of the columns, which determine the impression, but also as a whole. Just as the body of an animal or plant in nature grows freely and equally in all directions, so too the temple. The monumental peripteral temples with rectangular ground plans are not oriented in one direction, neither toward their sides nor their ends, as Egyptian temples and Christian churches are, and for this reason they do not have a dominating façade. For cult reasons, and because of the direction of the light when the sun is low, they are almost without exception laid out so that the two narrow, pediment ends face east and west. The altar lies before the eastern end, and a door there leads into the interior of the cella. In spite of this, the two ends are as little differentiated from one another as are the two sides. The building rests in itself, and is equally weighted in all directions. This is the basis, to no small degree, of its corporeity, and is what

139

makes it seem related in essence to the free-standing statue. In it, too, we recognize that the peculiar talent of the Greek artist lies in the plastic.

Fig. 120 This plastic corporeity of Greek buildings, carried to its logical extreme, led to the development of the circular structure, the tholos. The round building made far greater demands on the stonemason than the rectangular one, and required a high degree of skill in stone cutting. That these difficulties were tackled at all shows how urgently a definite artistic desire was seeking expression in this architectural form. The round building as a large independent structure first appeared among the Greeks. Following the prototype of the peripteral temple, a ring of columns was placed around the cylindrical cella. In those that have been preserved, for example the tholos at Delphi, the columns were of the Doric order, up into the classical period. Along with the pyramids of Egypt, this form of building is one of the purest abstractions of all architecture, since its ground plan embodies the most perfect geometric figure, the circle. But, in contrast to the absolute stereometry of the pyramids, these round peristyle buildings reveal clearly the predominantly plastic character of Greek architecture. The spatial element, for which the successors to Greek round buildings, notably the Roman Pantheon, were famous, is here completely undeveloped. Greek architects did not apply the same creative powers to the spatial as they did to the body of the buildings and its structural members. The Greek language, characteristically, has no fitting expression for what we understand by 'space'; they had to use a negative phrase.

The column is the constituent element of the peripteral building, and we think immediately of colonnades when the subject of Greek architecture comes up. The Greeks for the first time developed the column to its full potential: a form so independent and complete in itself that it can stand alone as a monument, and at the same time so adaptable that it can be allied with others of its kind to make a series so perfect that, seeing it, we believe that the column can be appreciated only in the harmony of such an ensemble. The articulated form of the Greek column directly expresses its static function. It is not only a practical physical support; it is the capacity for supporting, given an independent shape. The Greek column is a physical, self-sufficient form – and if this description sounds as if it were applied to something human, we find that it is appropriate when we see how the figures of maidens, Fig. 129 caryatids, sometimes take the place of columns, as in some Delphic treasuries and the Caryatid Portico (Porch of the Maidens) of the Erechtheum.

In contrast to the great diversity of pillars and plant-columns in Egyptian architecture, the Greek is limited to a few basic forms – in general, through all the centuries, to only two, the Doric and the Ionic. The 'Aeolic' capital is a special creation of the archaic, too much endebted to exotic oriental influence to be viable among the Greeks. The Corinthian capital does not appear until the late classic period; the imitation of plant forms makes it adaptable for varied decorative effects, and assured it a place in the age of 'art' and in the future. It hides the supporting core behind a pleasing outward appearance and ornamental splendor.

120   *Tholos, Delphi. Marble.*

In the Erechtheum we can see, not only the ashlar wall, but also Ionic columns in their classic, completely articulated form; in the North Hall they have already reached an over- Fig. 121 ripe stage of development. The base, which is a member of every Ionic as well as every Corinthian column, here consists of two tori (rounded swellings) with a scotia (groove) between, in the Attic manner. The upper torus is ornamented all over with a rich twisted band, which alternates between two different varieties. The joy in ornamentation toward the end of the fifth century also gave rise to the broad decorative band between the rounded Fig. 130 end of the fluting and the capital. The building in general is very rich in ornamental flourishes. The Ionic capital when used for the peristyle of a temple, as in the case of this three-sided porch, proves to be less adaptable than the Doric, because it does not offer the same aspect from all four sides. Instead, the two main sides are differentiated from the two less important by the typical Ionic volutes. Therefore, by its very nature, a row of Ionic columns needs a different kind of conclusion at the two ends, something which neutralizes the subsidiary sides of the capitals and brings a uniform appearance to the colonnade. For this purpose the arrangement of Ionic columns which encloses the Sarcophagus of the Mourning Women at Sidon has pilasters at the four corners. If the builder wants to use Ionic columns at the corners, in the same fashion as the uniform Doric peristyle, he is faced with the difficulty of making two adjoining sides of the capital both main views. This leads to a compromise solution, a diagonal capital, in which a volute with two faces is drawn out diagonally on

121 *Erechtheum. Acropolis, Athens. Marble.*

the outside corner, and the volute on the inside is bent in at right angles. It is quite clear from this that the classic Greek idea of the peripteral temple could not have emanated from the Ionic order, and must have been based on the Doric.

In contrast to the Ionic order, which is characterized by slender columns and a light openness, the Doric has a sturdy robustness; the ancients compared the Doric column to the male, the Ionic to the female, figure. The Doric column does not have an ornamental base; instead, its broad foot stands directly and powerfully on the pavement. Its flutings are shallower than the semicircular Ionic flutings, and join in a sharp ridge (arri), while the Ionic are separated by a narrow fillet; they lack a rounded conclusion at top and bottom, and disappear gradually at the capital. The shaft of the Doric column, which is more strictly limited in its relationships of height and thickness, tapers from the bottom up, to a greater or less degree, not at an unchanging rate, but slowly at first and then more rapidly. This tension, or entasis, the purpose of which is to support the heavy load of the entablature, has in it something of the nature of the play of muscles in a body which is tensed and standing firm. In the capital, consisting of a dish-shaped echinus and a square abacus of about the same height, these functional elements of support and load are given concentrated expres-

122   *Enneastylos, Paestum. Limestone.*

sion. The echinus summons up the shaft's tension to its greatest dynamic force, and discharges this energy against the counterpressure of the abacus, which it underpins, and which conveys the weight of the architrave into the capital. In the course of evolution from the archaic to the classical period, the basic form of the Doric capital is modified in characteristic fashion. At the beginning the load seems almost too heavy for the echinus to bear, and it looks as though it were almost pressed flat, as seen in the Enneastylos of Paestum. Later the   Fig. 122
outline becomes more severe and taut; and finally it rises agilely and effortlessly to meet   Fig. 120
the abacus.

In the triglyph frieze of the Doric entablature we recognize the previous constructional   Fig. 123
articulation of the building, left over from the time when it was erected in wood. The
triglyphs correspond to the ends of the ceiling beams, which were masked with small protective boards. The openings between the ends of the beams were closed with metopes
which, in a wooden building, were terra-cotta plates. These metopes might be painted or,
when they came to be made of stone, were decorated with reliefs, or else simply left blank,
as they were on the Temple of Poseidon at Paestum. The convincing effect of the triglyph
frieze in the total structure of the Doric peripteral temple depends principally on the fact that

they were not freely invented for artistic reasons, but instead were the natural result of practical considerations of workmanship. Their meaning is self-explanatory when we consider the orderly relationships of the parts of the structure to one another. Someone passing aesthetic judgment on the Doric order might point out how advantageously the triglyph frieze takes up and assimilates the two main factors in the façade, the rising of the columns and the repose of the architrave, and echoes them in the lively alternation of narrow triglyphs and broad metope surfaces; how the rhythm of the columns and the spaces between them is doubled, with two units of triglyph and metope taking up the same space as one column and the interval to the next; how the rhythm is accelerated once more above the triglyph frieze, in the under side of the cornice, where it is doubled again in the series of notched plates, the mutules, and the spaces between them, the viae; and finally, how the regulae along the top molding of the architrave announce in advance the position of the triglyphs and provide a vertical unity, and how the series of guttae in the mutules repeats the number of guttae in the regulae. Although this is all carefully thought out, it is not arbitrarily established; instead, it developed from the original requirements of good workmanship, and it serves to make clear the articulation of the architectural organism.

Fig. 124   This abundance of relationships, this similarity between the structural elements and the limbs of a body, is a part of a harmony of proportions in the total structure of the Doric temple, which can be seen at the height of its classic development in the pediment side of the Temple of Zeus at Olympia. This harmony is easily recognized in the strict regularity of the simple numerical proportions by which it may be expressed. Perhaps a sketch will

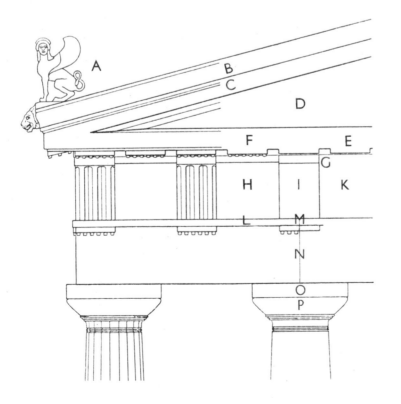

123   *Doric entablature.*

A	Acroterion
B	Sima
C	Slanting cornice
D	Tympanum
E	Cornice
F	Mutule
G	Via
H	Metope
I	Triglyph
K	Frieze
L	Taenia
M	Regula
N	Architrave
O	Abacus
P	Echinus

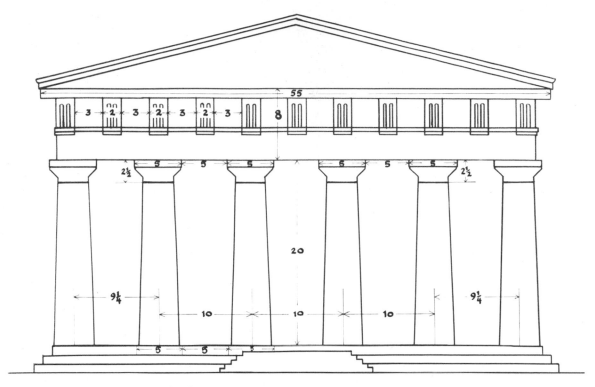

124   Pediment end of the Temple of Zeus, Olympia. Proportions.

explain more clearly the relationships that sound all too abstract in words. We find the proportion of 1:1 in the heights of echinus and abacus, as well as in the width of the abaci and the spaces between them; 1:2 in the height of the capitals and the space between the abaci, and also in the height of the columns and the width between their axes; 2:3 in the width of triglyphs and metopes; 2:5 in the height of the entablature and the height of the columns. In these proportions we find a counterpart to the Pythagorean theory, which held numbers to be the fundamental concepts of existence, and their pure relationships an image of the harmony of the universe.

The peristyle surrounds the inner building, the cella. To maintain the independence and stability of both, and at the same time to bind them together, is the principal problem in designing the ground plan of the Doric temple. Its classic solution is represented by the Temple of Zeus at Olympia. The bays of the peristyle are equal, both on the sides and on Fig. 125 the ends of the building, except for the corner bays which, for technical reasons, must be shortened, if the triglyphs and metopes are to remain the same width throughout. The normal width of the bay has a definite relationship to the width of the cella, which here, as in most cases, equals the width of three bays. Then the outer edges of the cella's longitudinal walls are aligned respectively with the axis of the second front column on both sides, counting from the corner. On the ends, the hall of the peristyle is made deeper, and this is done by aligning the east and west faces of the cella with the center of the second bay on the long side of the peristyle. In the Temple of Poseidon at Paestum, which was built somewhat later than the Temple of Zeus at Olympia, and exhibits several peculiarities of lower Italian

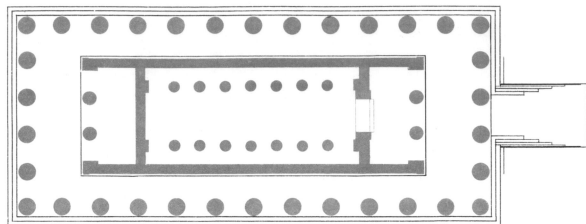

Ground plan of the
Temple of Zeus, Olympia.

Fig. 118, 119   origin, the illustrations show clearly how the cella was thus tied in to the peristyle, and how
at the same time the two structural units remained independent. In the peristyle of the
Temple of Zeus at Olympia there are six columns on the end to thirteen on the side, counting the corner columns each time. Six to eleven or six to thirteen – that is, one more or
one less than twice the number of end columns – is the classic proportion. The Temple of
Poseidon at Paestum has fourteen side columns to six end columns, but this more extended
ground plan is one of its lower Italian characteristics.

    The cella of the Temple of Zeus at Olympia shows the customary form of ground plan.

Fig. 117   It looks like a doubled *in-antis* building, of the same kind as the Treasury of the Athenians at
Delphi, but with this difference, that there is a back entrance, the opisthodomus, as well as
a porch at the eastern end, the pronaos. Both have two columns between the antae, and thus
look exactly alike, as do the two ends of the peristyle – illustrating the lengths to which
the Greeks went to obtain that balance between the opposites of a temple which we have
already mentioned. The sole difference in the entrance end occurs where a door leads from

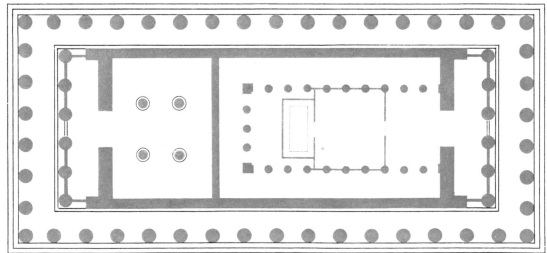

126   *Ground plan of the*
Parthenon. Acropolis, Athens.

146

127   Parthenon. Acropolis, Athens. Marble.

the pronaos into the interior of the cella; the back wall of the opisthodomus is unbroken. The interior of the cella is separated into three naves by two rows of columns, which support the roof. In the Poseidon Temple at Paestum we can still see today a similar interior division of the cella. There we find rows of Doric columns, smaller in diameter and height than the pillars of the peristyle and porches, standing in two stories, one on top of the other. Because of the great height of the interior, a single row of columns would have become too big, since the diameter increases with the height. When the architect did not want to use such a two-storied arrangement of smaller columns in a Doric interior, as was the case in the west room of the Parthenon and in the Propylaea on the Athenian Acropolis, he found a way out by using the Ionic column, with its slenderer and less strictly regulated proportions; but this intrusion of an element from another order does violence to the severe form structure of the Doric order. However, after the height of the classic period, such liberties became more frequent.

147

Fig. 126, 127

Fig. 125 If we compare the ground plan of the Parthenon with the classic ground plan of the Temple of Zeus at Olympia, we are struck with several peculiarities which bring home the fact that the builders of the Parthenon, at the time of the greatest blossoming of Athens under Pericles, were attempting something extraordinary: to raise a memorial for all time to this flourishing of Athens. The temple is especially imposing, with the unusually large column count of eight to seventeen in its peristyle. For the cella, the usual form of a doubled *in-antis* building was not sufficient. The side walls of the pronaos and opisthodomus are slightly shortened, thereby gaining room on both ends for a row of six columns placed in front of the cella. This makes the inner house of the temple hexastyle amphiprostyle. The cella consists of not one, but two inner rooms, with no communicating door. The western room has its own door leading from the back porch. This increases the equilibrium of the temple's two ends by still a third degree. The western room has four of the Ionic columns which we have already mentioned. The main room is divided in the more usual way into three naves with Doric columns in a two-storied arrangement, but here the columns also traverse the end, making a horseshoe shape. This provides a magnificent setting for the cult-image of Athena Parthenos, from the hand of Phidias. The purpose of the cella is to hold the cult-image, and thus to be the dwelling place of the divinity. (It is not a congregational room, as in a Christian church; the services of the cult are carried on outside, at the altar in front of the eastern pediment.) The cella alone would suffice for this purpose; the surrounding columns bestow on the venerated cult-image an atmosphere of preciousness, splendor, and respect.

A simple amphiprostyle, corresponding to the cella of the Parthenon, and not surrounded by a peristyle, is found among the buildings from the height of the classic period on the Fig. 128 Acropolis at Athens, the small temple of Athena Nike. It was first erected between 427 and 424, after the Parthenon, and did not receive the last of its plastic decoration until about 405, not long before the blossoming of Athens was suddenly cut short by the unfortunate outcome of the Peloponnesian War. It has a row of four graceful Ionic columns in front of the entrance to its small cella, and another row of four at the back. Their bases are an early Attic type, with a very low bottom torus, and a correspondingly higher central scotia. As in the Erechtheum, the architrave has three steps. The frieze around the temple is provided with reliefs.

Fig. 99, 121, 129 An Ionic building of quite unusual shape is to be seen in the Erechtheum. Only when seen from the east does it have the appearance of a hexastyle prostyle; all the rest is without precedent. Its irregular shape is explained by the builders' regard for cult tradition and the ancient sacred tokens which were connected with the site: the trident and salt-water spring of Poseidon, the sacred olive tree of Athena, the grave of Kekrops, and the cult of Athena Polias. The steepness of the land also made the site a difficult one. The architects' intention was a restorative one, which also operated at the same time in the retrenchment of the

138 *Temple of Athena Nike. Acropolis, Athens. Marble.*

grandiose building plan for the Propylaea. Mnesicles, its builder, wanted to glorify the
citadel sanctuary by means of a splendid, ceremonial entrance structure, and his desire was
so strong that he had no misgivings about disregarding, in his plans for the Propylaea, an
older cult installation which stood in his way. But the guardians of traditional piety proved
to be stronger, and the outbreak of the Peloponnesian War played its part in preventing
the realization of his plans. The architect of the Erechtheum, on the contrary, placed his
art completely in the service of cult interests, and what he achieved in so doing merits the
highest admiration. He created entirely new forms, such as the open north porch, four
columns wide and two columns deep, which we have already observed, and the southern
porch, the Caryatid Portico, consisting of six maidens in peplos, standing on a high socle
and supporting a delicate entablature. The various parts are nevertheless brought together
in a highly successful equilibrium, not by means of symmetry, for which the conditions are
lacking, but through a sort of architectonic counterpoise, in which large, open shapes are

149

Fig. 130 contrasted with small, heavy ones. In addition to the rich ornamentation of the bases and necks of the columns in the north hall, which we have already observed, there is a splendid series of palmettes crowning the surface of the walls. 'It is of decisive significance that the Ionic set of forms, in sharpest contrast to the Doric, has the capacity for receiving an ornament and developing it, determined only by artistic considerations, without any relationship to the structural elements.'[15] It is fitting to call the structure of the Erechtheum a work of art, in regard to both the design and the ornamental richness, in the sense of both spontaneity of invention and the satisfaction of aesthetic requirements. It embodies a tragic irony in the architecture of Greek temples: the time-honored basic form of the peripteral temple has to be abandoned, in order to validate ancient cult traditions; and, out of regard for the requirements of piety, new, freely manipulated means are made available to the artist. In other words, the very regard for pious requirements gives free play to the artistic. The Erechtheum was built in the first interval of peace during the Peloponnesian Wars, in the years following 421. This was still the half-century that is considered the height of the classic period, but it had already begun to decline, and the 'beautiful classic' was making itself felt. In all fields of the creative spirit at that time, we observe a surging forward of the artistic, an approach toward virtuosity. 'One does not remain long at the peak of circumstances,' reads a painfully true maxim of Goethe's.

129 *Caryatid Portico of the Erechtheum. Acropolis, Athens. Marble.*

ARCHITECTURAL SCULPTURE

Painting and sculpture accompany the pure architecture of temples and treasuries. Early Greek architecture, no less than early sculpture, was brightly colored. Color served the requirements of clear articulation and visibility. Here we shall discuss only that painting and sculpture which had something to say that was not expressed in the architecture itself, which was more than merely an ornamental accessory to the building, no matter to what an extent it may have improved the appearance of the structure. In Doric architecture, the

151

metopes may carry reliefs, and the area of the pediments may be filled with relief or with groups of sculptured figures. In early times painting was also used to fill the pediments as well as the metopes. It is significant that these are not supporting members of the building, for the clearness of the functional structure may not be obscured in a Doric building, as it frequently is, in various ways, in buildings of the Ionic order. The unchangeable, and not always convenient, areas of the rectangular metopes and the triangular pediments made unusual demands on the Greek sculptor in the way of composition, requiring the formal ability to fit figures into the assigned picture area, and the imagination to arrive at a meaningful scenic invention into which the parts could be ordered to make a whole.

Fig. 131–133   The oldest Greek pediment group known in its entirety is that of the Temple of Artemis at Korkyra (Corfu), which a Corinthian master created around 590. A huge image of a Gorgon dominates the center of the pediment. We have already become familiar with the Gorgon as a sign to ward off evil, and her appearance here has the same meaning. We know that in one of the oldest temples at Selinus in Sicily, a gigantic Gorgon's mask was placed alone in the empty field of the pediment. This temple was not nearly as old as the Temple of Artemis at Korkyra, but the use of a Gorgon's mask by itself in a temple pediment is certainly a very ancient custom. An uncanny power is ascribed to her: she excites terror, wards off evil, and serves as an apotropaic sign to protect the temple. We gain an idea of her effectiveness from the conclusion of the eleventh book of the Odyssey. When Odysseus wanted to question the souls of the dead at the entrance of the underworld, he was seized with fear 'lest the high goddess Persephone should send the head of the Gorgon, that dread monster, from out of Hades,' and he hastened back to his ship and ordered his men with all speed to loose the hawsers.

130   *Ornament from the Erechtheum. Acropolis, Athens. Marble.*
131 and 132   *Gorgon. Zeus striking down a giant. Pediment of the Temple of Artemis, Korkyra (Corfu). Poros.*

133   Pediment end of the Temple of Artemis, Korkyra (Corfu).

A separate Gorgon's mask also occurs among the oldest metopes, painted terra-cotta metopes from the Temple of Apollo at Thermos, erected during the last quarter of the seventh century. Still further examples might be added, confirming the use of the Gorgon's mask in very early times as an apotropaic sign on temples.

In the pediment of the Temple of Artemis at Korkyra, she is no longer simply a mask. A complete Gorgon is represented, with her knees bent in impetuous running. Large wings grow from her shoulders, and she wears giant winged shoes on her feet; two snakes girdle her waist, and snakes shoot out at both sides of her neck. Her frightening appearance is immensely effective; and yet, this Gorgon is no longer exclusively an apotropaic sign. The imagination of the archaic period has spun a myth around her. It is said that the boy Chrysaor and the winged horse Pegasus sprang from her body when daring Perseus struck off her head. Larger and smaller fragments of Chrysaor and Pegasus are still to be detected at the two sides of the Gorgon; but the pediment at Korkyra does not show her killing, for that would have weakened the traditional force of the sign, while the miraculous birth of the children from her blood only increases her power to frighten. Additional guardians endowed with primeval force are the two lion-panthers, one on each side of the central group, in heraldic fashion, with their heads turned outward like masks. These guardian animals are followed by a complete change in idea, for the two corners of the pediment tell legends in compressed form: on the left, Priam is threatened in the Trojan sanctuary by Neoptolemos, an excerpt from the Iliupersis, and on the right Zeus strikes down a giant

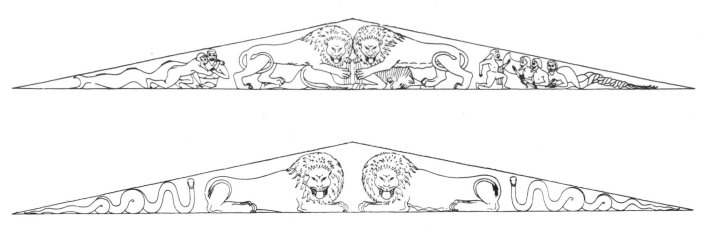

134 Pediments of the Old Temple of Athena. Acropolis, Athens.

with his bundle of thunderbolts. In the outermost points of the pediment, a lying man is still to be found on the left, and his counterpart probably once existed on the right. His posture, with head turned outward, indicates that he is a fallen warrior, perhaps, in spite of the difference in scale, supplementing the scene from the Iliupersis or, at the opposite end, the gigantomachy. Apparently there was no concern at all about unity of action in the pediment as a whole. Different things are placed independently side by side: apotropaic beings and miracles, animals on guard, along with violent events from the myths of gods and heroes. Power, which wards off all evil and subdues adversaries, seems to be the context that gives meaning to the pediment group as a whole. It is worthy of note, and probably not without significance, that Zeus, the father of gods and men, is inferior in size and position in the pediment to the Gorgon. He is subordinate to her, not in the divine order of greatness, for that does not come into question here, but in the reality pictured, where the potent sign was still stronger than the myth.

Fig. 134–136   The poros pediments of the Old Temple of Athena on the Athenian Acropolis are one or two decades more recent, and essentially different in kind. The Gorgon has vanished from the center of the pediment. She was apparently still indispensable, and found her place as an acroterion above the center of the pediment – for how long, we cannot say; we only know that in the fifth century something else served as the central acroterion. In the eastern pediment of the Old Temple of Athena the guardian animals, two lions, have pressed forward into the center, in a heraldic design, crouching watchfully and filled with assembled force. With them are two enormous looped snakes, with heads raised threateningly and gaping mouths, occupying the side slopes of the pediment area. These snakes have a direct connection with the divinity who inhabits the temple, Athena. Very ancient in origin, older than Athena herself, the citadel serpent who lived on the Acropolis has finally been subjugated to the goddess. This eastern pediment is still very similar to the older pediment at Korkyra, and even surpasses it in the avoidance of narrative scenes. But in the western pediment, even the symbolic has been transformed into an event: two lions occupy the center here, too, but they are not calm and watchful; instead, they furiously attack a cow. Myths are spread out to the right and left of this group of fighting animals, as they are in the pediment at Korkyra. On the left, Herakles is wrestling with the fish-bodied Old Man of the Sea, Nereus, presumably in order to learn from him the location of the garden with the golden apples of the Hesperides. On the right is a fabulous triple-formed creature with bearded human heads, broad masculine chests, and several intertwined serpent bodies. Judging from the symbols in the hands of this three-bodied monster, namely a bird, a flaming, and an undulating thing, he must have been an artist in transforming himself into airy, fiery, and fluid elements. From this we conclude that he must be the many-shaped Proteus, whom Menelaos, hastening up from the left (if tentative restorations are correct), was questioning as to the whereabouts of Helen, who had been mysteriously abducted.

The representation of events in this western pediment of the Old Temple of Athena requires a different means of expression from the symbolism of the pediment at Korkyra. In Korkyra the pediment group is a relief, very strongly raised up from the background, but still quite flat as a whole. The forms are made clear by graphic means, corresponding to the incision style of Corinthian vase painting, and the details are drawn. The lines still preserve geometric exactness: concentric circles drawn with a compass pattern the pelts of the lion-panthers, and a simple, large meander ornaments the step of the pediment. Although the pediment figures on the Old Temple of Athena are not yet completely plastic, they have a powerful plastic tension which fills their bodies, almost to bursting. Herakles wrestling with Nereus is swelled up with clenched muscular force, which brings the outline of the figure into motion. The drawing is subordinate to the modeling; and the painting, which has been better preserved in this poros sculpture than almost anywhere else, strengthens with its brightness the impression of fresh nature.

135 and 136   Herakles wrestling with Nereus. – Proteus(?). Corner figures in the western pediment of the Old Temple of Athena. Acropolis, Athens. Poros.

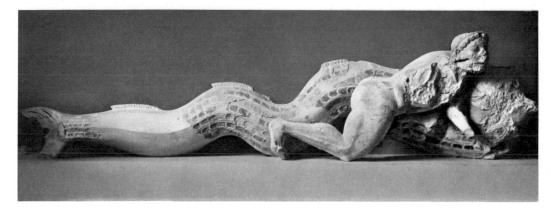 

137   Council of the gods. Eastern frieze on the Siphnian Treasury, Delphi. Marble. 64 cm. high.

In the middle and later parts of the sixth century, a unified theme prevailed in pediment groups. As in vase painting, it is usually a tale from the legends of gods and heroes, pictured in a self-evident incident.

Fig. 137–142 This type of late archaic architectural sculpture is represented here, not by a pediment group, but by the frieze of figures from the Siphnian Treasury at Delphi, which is of especially fine workmanship, and well preserved. On this Ionic *in-antis* building, with two caryatids between the antea of the entrance side, which faces west because of the rising land, a relief frieze runs around the four sides. One of the pediments contained a molded relief showing the theft of the Delphic tripod by Herakles, who sought to wrest the sacred vessel

138   Aphrodite, Artemis and Apollo. Detail of Fig. 137.

156

139   Battle between Greeks and Trojans. Eastern frieze on the Siphnian Treasury, Delphi. Marble. 64 cm. high.

away from Apollo – a tale that took place in Delphi itself and for that reason is especially appropriate. The visitor who approached the sanctuary from the east, walking along the sacred road, first caught sight of the eastern frieze. Today it can still be seen, almost com- Fig. 137–139 plete: to the left, an assembly of the gods, to the right, a battle before Troy. Battle chariots harnessed with teams of four have driven up and stand at the side, held by charioteers, where they enclose the central group symmetrically. Here armed warriors have begun a duel for the body of a fallen comrade. The fight is still equally balanced between the two combattants, for, on the left, the Olympian gods, as in Homer, have gathered in council in order to weigh the outcome. The gods who are friendly to the Trojans sit opposite from those who are

140   Team of four. Western frieze on the Siphnian Treasury, Delphi (detail). Marble. 64 cm. high.

141   *Gigantomachy. Northern frieze on the Siphnian Treasury, Delphi (detail). Marble. 64 cm. high.*

158

142 *Gigantomachy. Northern frieze on the Siphnian Treasury, Delphi (detail). Marble. 64 cm. high.*

143 Head of Athena from the newer eastern pediment of the Old Temple of Athena. Acropolis, Athens. Marble. Height of the whole figure, c. 180 cm.

against them, separated from one another. Zeus is enthroned on a precious chair in the center of the deliberating gods. To his left sit Apollo, youthful, lively and noble, his huntress sister Artemis, and the more voluptuous Aphrodite, both begging and entreating Apollo with gestures, and at the end, violent Ares with his armor and large, round shield. Across from them are the friends of the Achaeans, probably the first one, in the gap, Poseidon, next to him Athena, who is identified by her snake-rimmed aegis, and finally two goddesses, possibly Hera and Demeter.

160

144 *Herakles purifies the Augean stables. Metope. Eastern end of the cella of the Temple of Zeus, Olympia. Marble. 160 cm. high.*

The northern frieze of the Siphnian Treasury, facing the sacred road, shows a giganto- Fig. 141, 142 machy, a theme which we have already met in abbreviated form in Korkyra, and which fills a pediment of the Treasury of the Megarians in Olympia. For the late archaic sculptor, a gigantomachy offers many varied and exciting things to tell: how Hephaistos pushes and pulls the enormous bellows, how the lions from the team of Dionysos attack a fleeing giant, how Hera bends over her fallen opponent to deal the death blow with her lance, how giants hurl boulders – and much more, told in the most exact, relevant details.

Fig. 140The friezes on the other two sides are in such a ruined condition that definite interpretation is not possible, but we can recognize riders, chariots, teams of four, the rape of maidens, and in the west, perhaps the judgment of Paris. Both of these friezes, as well as the pediment, were executed by a different master from the sculptor of the eastern and northern friezes. The latter is especially skilled in the plastic completeness of the individual figures and their grouping; he understands how to mold the bodies and garments, rounding out and hollowing them in many intermediate stages. The other master, who also created the pediment and was therefore perhaps the chief sculptor, retains a flatter character in his friezes. This is seen especially clearly in his groups of horses, as distinguished from the teams of four in the Trojan battle scene. The elevations lie on top of one another in layers, parallel to the ground of the relief, and push out in front of one another. By this means the outlines are clear and definite, and the details are reproduced in fine lines, mainly by graphic rather than plastic means. These differences are known to exist in the work of Parian and of Naxian sculptors, and it is not inconceivable that the Siphnians commissioned artists from the neighboring islands of Paros and Naxos to carry out this pictorial decoration.

Just as the pediment of this treasury depicted a local legend, so it was appropriate for the pediment of a temple to show the divinity who inhabited it. This occurred more and more frequently in the last quarter of the sixth century. The Athenians wanted to replace the poros pediment of the Old Temple of Athena, made at the height of the archaic period, with a more modern and expensive marble pediment. For the western pediment, which already contained narrative scenes and myths, they were satisfied with a marble copy of the original. But on the eastern end they wanted to replace the symbolic lions and snakes with a more up-to-date gigantomachy. Athena, stepping out boldly and swinging her aegis with a mighty gesture of her left arm, with a fallen giant at her feet, was to occupy the Fig. 143center. Her head is of gripping beauty; it has much more seriousness and sublimity than is generally found in the late archaic period, and it seems to proclaim the spirit of a new age.

The chief works of this new period, that of the severe classic style, are the sculptures of the Fig. 144-153Temple of Zeus at Olympia, twelve metope reliefs and the groups of both pediments. As a theme for the metopes, it was natural to choose the labors of Herakles, since Herakles is directly connected with Olympia. It was here that the enormous stables of Augeas, the king of Elis, were situated, the stables which Herakles had to purify in one day, at enormous difficulty. Here also he is said to have measured off the stadium and instituted the Olympic games. The metopes that were to contain reliefs were not the many surrounding the outer building, but only six each above the pronaos and the opisthodomus. To fill them, the twelve labors of Herakles that are familiar to us were chosen and joined to make a cycle. Archaic painters and sculptors depicted more labors of Herakles than these twelve, although never the Elian adventure of cleansing the Augean stables. Since this very theme first appeared in Olympia and, from that time on, belonged to the cycle of twelve, there can be

145 *Head of Athena from the Lion metope. Western end of the cella of the Temple of Zeus, Olympia. Marble. Height of the metope, 160 cm.*

146   *Series of metopes on the western end of the cella of the Temple of Zeus, Olympia.*

no question that it was originally created in Olympia. The Elian adventure was to receive a preferred position on the entrance end of the temple; since it did not belong among the first adventures of Herakles, such as the killing of the Nemean lion, the cycle had to begin with the latter on the western end. Thus the sequence was surprisingly reversed, and ran from the back to the entrance side of the cella.

Fig. 144   The representation of the cleansing of the Augean stables had to be newly invented, and from it we can recognize directly the sculptor's nature and his way of looking at things. The picture shows none of the circumstantial details of which the legend tells – the great stables, the thousands of cattle, the enormous heaps of filth, the diverting of a great river to the task. It depicts only the strenuously active Herakles and his divine protectress, Athena. The exclusion of the inessential is a genuine Greek trait which we have frequently come across, but scarcely ever in such unconditional severity. Archaic painters did not hesitate to make use of pertinent adjuncts to the narration; but the master of Olympia is concerned solely with the conduct and bearing of the human being. Herakles is in the act of wielding an implement, the shaft of which he grasps with both hands. His legs far apart, his weight rests solidly on his right leg, while he braces himself powerfully with the left; this brings his trunk far forward, and both arms are drawn back. With the direction of the action pointing toward the left, the backward motion of the arms provides an inner equilibrium. As in Myron's discus thrower, the sculptor has seized that pregnant moment when action, passing over into counteraction, comes to a halt and, as at the height of a pendulum's swing, the force is strained to the utmost, and at the same time is at rest. In the figure of Herakles, the counter-balance of the widely extended body is almost blatant; but in the form of Athena behind him, the counterpoise is gently expressed in the differentiation between the leg which

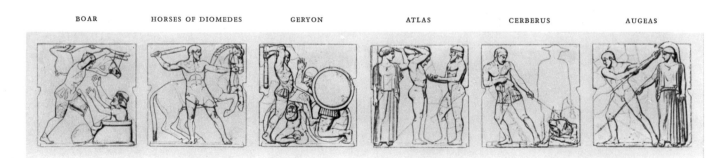

147   *Series of metopes on the eastern end of the cella of the Temple of Zeus, Olympia.*

supports her weight and the one which is at ease, and in the varied contours of the two sides of her body. In turn, both figures are balanced in relation to each other, in a powerful compensation of tensions, contrasting simplicity with multiplicity, rest with motion, composure with violence.

The master who designed these Herakles metopes again proves himself a unique personality when he depicts themes that have a long tradition behind them. On a black-figure vase painting, Herakles at the Stymphalian swamp encounters an enormous mass of swimming and flying water birds; but on the metope, his task already completed, he presents a handful of birds, as a symbol of the trial surmounted, to Athena, who sits waiting on a rock, and whose assistance has made possible his success. The head of this Athena is one of the most Fig. 149 beautiful and mature heads in the Olympia sculptures, and is not inferior to the soulful Athena head of the lion metope. When we compare them to the somewhat earthy Athena Fig. 145 head of the Atlas metope, we might take them for very close relatives, executed by a highly gifted and deeply sensitive sculptor. It is, of course, unthinkable that all the Olympia sculptures were carved by a single hand. Several co-workers and helpers must have assisted the master who designed and directed the work, even though it is difficult to differentiate them with any certainty.

In the design, on the other hand, we perceive the single, thoughtful spirit of a guiding master. In the lion metope he frees himself completely from the many traditional representations of Herakles wrestling with the lion. The dangerous adventure is over, and the Nemean lion lies dead on the ground. This severe classic interpretation differs from archaic representations of the theme in the same way that we have observed before: in place of the happening, the inner participation of the hero is depicted, his perception of deed and task. In contrast to all the other metopes, Herakles is represented here as youthful and unbearded.

148   Central group from the eastern pediment of the Temple of Zeus, Olympia. Marble. 330 cm. high.

His head rests heavily on his propped right hand, and this introspective pose seems to express clearly the idea that he is entering upon a decision to live a life of effortful action.

Fig. 146, 147   We can tell that the separate Herakles metopes belong together, not only from their consecutive content, but also because of the composition. The six in each group, which meet the eye simultaneously, are related compositionally to one another and form a unified whole. This can be seen clearly in the series of eastern metopes. Carrying on his shoulder the boar of Erymanthos, which he has hunted down, Herakles threatens to hurl the captured beast at the king Eurystheus, who has crawled into a pithos and stretches out his arms in pleading. This starts a continuing motion from left to right with such powerful impact that Herakles almost topples over the fugitive Eurystheus. In the next metope, that of the steeds of Diomedes, the motion toward the center of the row is carried on in a broadly flowing manner by the rearing horse, while Herakles, although facing in the same direction, blocks the flow slightly by reining in the animal. In the adjoining picture of the battle with the three-bodied monster, Geryon, Herakles' body is stretched to the utmost tension, like a bow, as he raises his arms with a club, which runs parallel to the vertical edge of the picture, to strike his three-bodied opponent. In the monster's collapse, the motion toward the right disintegrates, like a stream flowing into a bubbling whirlpool. Thus, just before the center of the row, the motion from left to right is brought to a standstill. This center, which is at the same time the central axis of the building itself, needs stability and careful consideration; it may not be overplayed. It is immediately emphasized at the right by the Atlas metope, constructed of three column-like figures. The severe sobriety of the Atlas metope is intentionally contrasted to the violent confusion of the Geryon metope; it imposes an incontestable barrier to the motion from left to right. Its calm steadfastness is all the more necessary because, in the last two metopes there is also a powerful motion surging toward the center. It begins at the far right with Herakles' stormy position of attack in the Augeas metope, and continues, less forcefully but with straining tension, in the metope between, where Herakles, pulling toward the left, draws Cerberus out of the underworld. The last three metopes, like the first two, form a well-balanced and ordered half, and the two Athenas, calmly facing one another, serve as end pillars. The Cerberus metope, balanced between calm and violence, fulfills the same function in the right half of the series as the Diomedes metope in the left. The whole row is firmly integrated by means of symmetry, contrast, and correspondence between the parts.

The pillar-like Athena of the Augeas metope affirms the fact that, with her, the sequence of all twelve metopes has been brought to an end. At the beginning of the entire series, in the lion metope, there is a corresponding Athena who, in her original state, was probably also pillar-like. With clever calculation, the metope farthest to the right in the western series, the Amazon metope, is designed so that it does not form a conclusion; instead, it leads out beyond the row to the right, indicating that the continuation of the series is to be found in the eastern row. There is no need to explain in detail the careful balance and integration of the western metopes. Although this row, too, displays a masterly handling of artistic

149 *Head of Athena from the Stymphalian metope. Western end of the cella of the Temple of Zeus, Olympia. Marble. Height of the metope, 160 cm.*

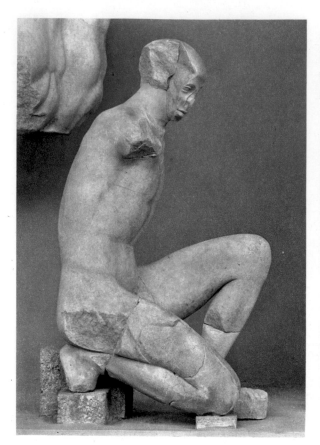

150 and 151   *Temple of Zeus, Olympia. Boy from the eastern pediment. 105 cm. high. – Lapithan woman from the western pediment. Marble. 165 cm. high.*

form, it does nothing more than express an intensification and deepening of the ancient mythology.

Fig. 148, 150, 152 Of the two pediments of the Temple of Zeus at Olympia, the pictorial content of the eastern one is also related meaningfully, in several ways, to the temple and the locality. Zeus, as the god of Olympia, dwells in the temple, and he governs the local games in his attribute as keeper of the oath. Oinomaos, who is preparing to undertake a race against Pelops with a team of four, is the mythical king of the region. The race itself can be considered a metaphor of the Olympic games. And finally, Pelops was honored as a hero in the sanctuary of Olympia. These are the main persons who appear in the eastern pediment. Oinomaos, with his wife Sterope, had promised his daughter, Hippodameia, to the suitor who could outrace him on a journey across the Peloponnesus to the altar of Poseidon on the Isthmus. He gave his opponents a head start, but made the dreadful condition that he would kill any with whom he caught up. When thirteen suitors had already met death in this manner, Pelops appeared as a wooer, trusting to the swifter-than-flight horses which he had requested from Poseidon, and had graciously been granted. The outcome of this dangerous undertaking was happy for Pelops, and fatal to Oinomaos, who was overtaken by death. The master designer concentrated this whole myth in the tense, expectant moment imme-

168

diately before the race. The fateful bargain for life and death has been sworn. Five erect forms fill the center of the pediment's triangle. Exactly in the center, between Pelops with Hippodameia on the left and Oinomaos with Sterope on the right, and towering a head above them, stands the mighty figure of Zeus. His head has been lost, but what remains of the neck indicates that it was turned to his right, toward Pelops, as though he 'bowed his dark brow' in promise (Iliad I 528). In his left hand he holds the thunderbolt with which, at the end, he will set in flames the palace of Oinomaos. The fact that he holds the thunderbolt in his left hand, instead of in his right as usual, and therefore on the side where Oinomaos stands, is intended as an exciting hint of what is to happen, as is the turning of his head. Zeus is not seen by those standing beside him, and they are turned away from him; but he is none the less actual and present. The sculptor, like Aeschylus, intends to express the idea that everything 'lies in the hands of the gods.'[16] The two couples, who correspond to one another in order to fill the shape of the pediment symmetrically, are so completely contrasted in details that each of the four mythical figures becomes an individual person: Oinomaos, in masculine maturity, a self-confident, aggressive ruler; Pelops, across from him, a handsome, well formed, supple, and enterprising youth; Sterope placing herself on view as queen, proudly, and a little arrogantly; the maiden Hippodameia, showing propriety and modesty, timid and thoughtful. Mutual inclination is expressed in the way in which Pelops and Hippodameia turn to each other. Oinomaos and Sterope, on the other hand, both appear to be oriented in the same direction, toward their extravagant aims, undaunted by the dictates of fate, which the two young people regard with pious awe.

The two chariots with their teams of four are in position. Pelops' horses, those presented by Poseidon, are restless and lively, ready for a quick departure. The driver is standing

Fig. 148

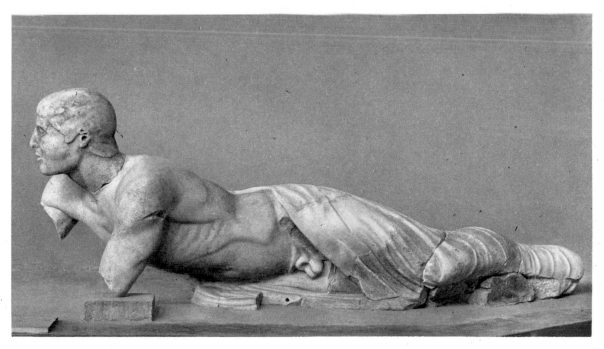

152 *Kladeos.*
Right corner of pediment of the eastern end of the Temple of Zeus, Olympia. Marble. 82.5 cm. high.

behind the chariot, prepared for an immediate start. The boy in front of the horses, probably from the retinue of Pelops, is busy with a final arrangement for his lord. Oinomaos' chariot, with the horses of Ares, waits calmly. The driver is not yet needed. Corresponding to Pelops' boy, a female servant kneels idly before Sterope, her activity completed. Two seers follow next, the ancestors of the two races of priests at Olympia. The seer on Pelops' side seems to be joyously moved, while the other, directly behind the team of Oinomaos, is worried with presentiments of evil. Near him squats a boy who is doing something to his big toe, indicating the matter-of-fact, easy-going attitude of everyone on the side of Oinomaos. In the two corners of the pediment there are figures of reclining men, again obviously contrasted in their bearing. According to ancient tradition they represent the two rivers which encompass the sanctuary of Olympia, placed in the pediment in conformity to their geographical locations: on the left, the broad-flowing Alpheios, and on the right the more rapid Kladeos. Thus, in the eastern pediment of the Temple of Zeus at Olympia, a number of local references are integrated into a meaningful unity and ever-present reality. In a moment of calm restraint, like the stillness before a storm, the extensive myth is powerfully held in check with the tension of conflicting forces.

Fig. 152

In the pictorial invention of this eastern pediment, the various kinds of earlier solutions to the problem of pediment decoration, after slow transformations and constant development, are carried to an almost unrivaled perfection, by incorporating the significance of the locality, and by objective concentration and compositional tension. The western pediment of the Temple of Zeus at Olympia, on the other hand, seems to have developed less decisively beyond the traditions of late archaic pediment groups. The mythical material presented there, the attack of wild centaurs on the Lapithae at the marriage feast of Pirithous, the friend of Theseus, is general in nature and seems to have little explicit relationship to the temple and the locality. But that is the only respect in which it seems somewhat old-fashioned; artistically it surpasses even the eastern pediment and the metopes, and there can be no doubt that a single master planned the sculptural decorations of the entire temple. Since it is his manner to work meaningfully with contrasts, he places stormy, passionately excited life in the western pediment, opposite the tension-charged restraint of the eastern. Only Apollo, as avenger of violated order and guardian of the right, stands in the center of the pediment, just as majestically and immovably as Zeus in the eastern pediment and, like Zeus, promises cessation of the outrage with the commanding and directing gesture of his right arm. For all the confusion of the surging press of battle, the rapes of maidens and boys, the suffering and resistance, attacking and forcing, the figures are arranged symmetrically in groups of three; two, three, and two, in both halves of the pediment; and the matching of the sequence of Lapithae, maidens and centaurs, as well as the placing of the individual figures, is carried astonishingly far. This symmetrical grouping and clear division into separate groups would nullify the unity of the pediment as a whole, if it were not for the concentration resulting from the attack of an up-raised hero next to the center in each half, and from the energetic pressing forward of the outermost Lapithae from the corners toward the center.

Fig. 151, 153

153 Head of a youth from the western pediment of the Temple of Zeus, Olympia. Marble.

Although the freedom of invention in the two pediments seems at first glance to be almost unbounded, actually the designing master does not indulge in arbitrary artistic license; rich as the Olympia sculptures are in the invention of characteristic figures and unique action motifs, haphazard reality finds no place. Instead, the master confines himself to the simple, basic forms of standing, striding, attacking, collapsing, squatting, kneeling, sitting, and

Fig. 150, 151 lying. In this connection, if we compare the kneeling boy of the eastern pediment with the Lapithan woman in the struggling group of the western pediment, we find, for all the differences of arm and head movements determined by the situation, that the basic posture of kneeling remains the same; the folds and drapery of the Lapithan woman's garments reveal the basic figure hidden beneath. Here, as in the free-standing statue, the plastic art of the severe classic style limits itself, with moderate freedom, to unambiguous, easily grasped statuary models, in which one motif is exhaustively expressed.

Of the great skill and empathic ability of the master's assistants in the plastic realization of his inventions, we cannot speak further; for, without having the warmth and radiance of the Parian marble before our eyes, we can scarcely gain a hint of the plasticity that exists in these incomparable marble bodies – or, even more, of what sculpture itself can be.

The Olympia sculptures, and most of the statues of the severe classic style, have such a powerful plastic effect because the perception of form is dominated by the sensuality of strong, full, tense curves. What is characteristic in the plastic feeling of a period or a master can be most easily recognized where the sculptor's natural inclination is not restricted by the subject matter, where he can express himself as freely as possible. Such pieces, characteristic of the severe classic manner, are found, for example, in the cushion which Herakles uses as a pad for his shoulders when he takes over the weight of the world from Atlas, a clever

Fig. 154 invention of the Olympia master, and in the cushion on which a hetaera sits playing the aulos, in the Ludovisi relief. In both cases, the sculptor takes advantage of the idea that counter-pressure results in a tight swelling and tension. The full curvature leaves no room for the concave along with the convex; instead of easy indentations, there are only violent constrictions, which act as clear, sharp boundaries underlining the corporeity. In both cases, the cushion can almost serve as a model of the severe classic style, a metaphor for the new inner spirit, the fulfilled body emanating power and soundness from within. The plastic, which was self-evident in the archaic period, is now to achieve self-realization; now it is not so much a natural potentiality as an actuality. This explains the special kind of plasticity of the statues of the fifth century.

A corresponding emanation of the spiritual marks the classic human image as revealed,

Fig. 155, 156 with heart-rending greatness, in the statue of a dying child of Niobe, which probably originally belonged to a pediment group from the period of the Parthenon sculptures. The daughter of Niobe has been fatally struck by the arrow of the avenging Artemis, as punishment for her mother's effrontery. The wounded girl has lifted both arms, reaching involun-

154 *Hetaera playing the aulos. Throne of Ludovisi. Marble. 104 cm. high.*

tarily toward the place behind her shoulders where the goddess' destroying arrow has hit her, and she has fallen to her knee. Her body, which rises beautifully from the flowing intricacy of the falling drapery, is not yet marked by death, and no passionate outburst of pain or sorrow at being snatched away from life in the springtime of her years distorts her face. Her inexpressibly soulful gaze is turned calmly and trustingly toward the heavenly ones, in whose hands lies everything, both life and fate. She pays with her life for a guilt not her own. She does not offer a 'tragically' ineffectual resistance to the necessary and inevitable fate; rather, in the limited freedom of her ending existence, she accepts the divine dispensation. As she meets destruction, she comes completely to herself. At the boundary of her life she achieves a full measure of self-realization and the fulfillment of her humanity. In this extraordinary human truth lies the greatness and beauty of the work.

PHIDIAS

Wᴇ HEN THE time is ripe, the lot falls to one outstanding genius to condense in his work everything that the period has previously achieved in varied multiplicity, to see in a unified fashion the separate objects of the experienced and imagined world, and to shape them into a whole. At the end of the Middle Ages, this was Dante's mission; at the height of the Greek classic period, it was the destiny of Phidias. Pericles, so we are told, assigned to Phidias the task of supervising the renovation of the Acropolis; since he is known only as a sculptor, we may assume that the sculptural ornamentation of the Parthenon was his actual work. But, however his assignment may have read, or whatever theme may have been supplied to him, it was certainly his all-embracing intellect which thought out, alone, the whole scope and enormous multiplicity of the subject matter, designed the unified plan for presenting it, drew up the arrangement and grouping, sketched the figures in advance, and, with his own hands, fashioned a few of the statues in the most important locations. Polykletos, at the same time, perfected in his work the image of the human being, the essence of man as he is, pure and undisguised; Phidias, in his work, achieved the same kind of image of the Greek cosmos.

Fig. 157–166   In the Parthenon, the architectural splendor is matched by an extraordinary wealth of

174

sculptures. At the height of the archaic period, the two pediments of the Old Temple of Athena on the Acropolis had already been filled with completely plastic groups; the Parthenon repeated this manner of filling the pediments, but on a vast scale and with incomparable grandeur. At the end of the archaic epoch, the Athenians had decorated their treasury in Delphi with the grand number of thirty relief metopes, surrounding the building; on the giant structure of the Parthenon there were a total of ninety-two metopes on all four sides of the peristyle, all of them sculptured with figures in relief. In buildings of the Ionic order, such as the Siphnian Treasury at Delphi, a relief frieze ran around the entablature in place of the Doric triglyph frieze; in the Parthenon, this was taken over into the Doric order, as an innovation, and a tremendously long relief frieze encircled the cella, including the prostyle column arrangement. Nor should we forget the lion heads at the corners, the acroteria set on the gables, and the gold and ivory cult-image of Athena Parthenos in the cella.

On the metopes was depicted, in battles of former times, the securing of the ordered world, the cosmos of the Greeks; in the pediments, the appearance and dominion of the eternal Olympian gods, especially in regard to Athens; and in the frieze, a festive self-portrait of the people of Athens, the polis, caught in a solemn moment, lifted above the everyday, and preserved for the ages. The procession on the Parthenon frieze is the culmination of those representations of ceremonial life which began with funeral scenes on the geometric grave vessels.

The metope reliefs on all sides of the peristyle are unified, both in composition and, on three sides at least, in subject matter. Battles between Athenians and Amazons occupy the western side – that is, the side that looks out over the hill of Ares, from which the combative daughters of Ares, the Amazons, besieged the Acropolis. This is one of many references to the locality, a feature in which the master of the Parthenon surpassed even the master of Olympia. The motion proceeds in the customary manner from left to right, and the sequence of pictures is arranged in a simple rhythm, with metopes showing mounted Amazons alternating with those fighting on foot. This is carried through so regularly that no attempt is made to close the open right end of the row compositionally, with some sort of counter-motion. Perhaps this is meant to lead over to the southern metopes, to compensate for the motion in the frieze, which proceeds in the opposite direction, around the left corner to the north.

The northern metopes were purposely destroyed in very early times, when the Parthenon was transformed into the church of Hagia Sophia. Only the metope at the western corner, showing Hera seated and Athena approaching her, escaped this fate, because the Christians interpreted it as Mary and the angel of the annunciation, and therefore spared it. Later the gunpowder explosion of 1687 tore an obliterating gap in this row, as well as in the southern row. Therefore we cannot form a conception of the design as a whole, and know only that it depicted the conquering of Ilium by the Greeks, with the deciding council of the gods probably shown in the three western metopes.

155   *Head of one of Niobe's dying children. Detail of Fig. 156.*

The metopes on the southern side, a large number of which still remain, are the best preserved of all the Parthenon metopes, and the central ones, which were destroyed, can be judged by old drawings. Here were depicted battles between the Lapithae and the centaurs, and also a local Attic myth which glorifies as an Athenian, the hero Ion, who gave his name to the Ionians. The eight central metopes are devoted to scenes from this legend, and are flanked on each side with twelve centaur metopes. Thus, in content and in composition, the result is a lucid and artistic triptychal arrangement – something new in a metope series, although it had always been natural in pediment groups, with their emphasized center. The central metopes, more or less statuesque in character, are contrasted to the side wings, with their lively scenes of action, centaur battles and the rape of maidens. The eight metopes in the center are clearly divided, both in form and content, into two groups of two each, and one of four; while each group of twelve centaur metopes is skillfully linked together by means of motifs showing youths winning and losing, attacking and defending, facing the same direction and turning against their adversaries, these motifs changing from plate to plate or within smaller groups of metopes. Those to the left are once again divided triptychly.

176   156   *Dying child of Niobe. Marble. 149 cm. high.*

157 *Centaur metope. Southern side of the Parthenon. Acropolis, Athens. Marble. 134 cm. high.*

Fig. 157, 158   In the centaur metopes, the battle between shapely youths and monsters of the wilderness surges back and forth inexorably. Uninfluenced by sympathy for beings of his own kind and custom, the master of the Parthenon, with courageous magnanimity and insight, allows the balance to tremble between victory and defeat through all the fighting groups. Knowing the limits of the human sphere in the face of divine necessity, his imagination soars to a lofty viewpoint, where fates tremble in the scales of Zeus. The series begins with a wonderful metope, still to be found on the building, in which a young Lapith holds off a mighty centaur with bold daring, although his neck is already in the deadly embrace of his opponent's left arm; already forfeit to death, in this preserved moment of utmost tension he remains indestructibly victorious. Radiating courage, individual youths press in upon cen-

178

158 *Centaur metope. Southern side of the Parthenon. Acropolis, Athens. Marble. 134 cm. high.*

taurs, push them back, and force them to the ground. The Olympia master, in his Herakles cycle, continually had something new to tell, from one metope to the next; but in these centaur metopes the designer limits his subject matter to a single motif, the duel of a youth with a centaur; in the place of a rich variety of inventions, he substitutes inexhaustible variations on a single theme. The Parthenon master is concerned, not so much with the event, as with the individual's manifold and infinitely varied ways of conducting himself in the face of a fate that remains the same. One of his most magnificent pictorial inventions (magnificent too in execution, and considered to be definitely a work from Phidias' own hand[17])   Fig. 158 shows a youth who has just expired, lying on the ground, while a centaur rears triumphantly over him. In metope pictures such as this, the 'tragic age of the Greeks' found classic

159 *Dionysos. Eastern pediment of the Parthenon. Acropolis, Athens. Marble. 121 cm. high.*

expression, just as it did in the poetry of its greatest tragedian, Sophocles, in which suffering has acquired 'the character of an aspect of fate imprisoning man.'[18]

Only the gods achieve victory without suffering or death, in their battle against the giants, depicted in the eastern metopes. Here almost all of the twelve highest gods face their opponents in duel. Exactly in the center, Zeus fights while Hera drives his team; to the left is Poseidon with Amphitrite, and to the right Apollo with Artemis as his charioteer. Thus the six central metopes form a predominating, homogeneous, and unified group, and the high rank of the gods fighting there gives it a special importance. The four metopes on each side, to the left and right, remain as wings, once again presenting a plainly triptychal arrangement. The central group is unmistakably bracketed by symmetrically placed teams of horses, and a caesura is brought about by counter-motion in the side metopes directly adjacent to it. A team at the extreme right, that of Helios, powerfully brings the whole sequence to a halt, through its motion toward the center. More refined divisions and connections are added to the composition. While the Olympia master obtained his effects in the Herakles sequence chiefly by means of direct contrasts and strongly opposed tensions, the Parthenon master, with a different conception of order, prefers an interlocking triad to an opposed duality. He minimizes contrasts by allowing the center to dominate and by subordinating the two wings. The designer is concerned with balance and with the harmony of a well-articulated unity, here as well as in the frieze and the pediments.

160   *Aphrodite. Eastern pediment of the Parthenon. Acropolis, Athens. Marble. 100 cm. high.*

Most of the sculptures from the two pediment groups have been destroyed. We can gain an idea of their condition in the year 1674, when they were already incomplete, from the so-called Carrey drawings. They do not enable us to imagine the whole of the eastern pediment, since at that time only the extreme angles were still in existence. The sculptures there have been preserved into our own day. All we know of the great center is that it depicted the birth of Athena. Zeus, enthroned as the father of the gods, and Athena, brought by him motherless into the world, occupied the center of the pediment, and the highest Olympian gods were grouped around them, marveling at the unprecedented miracle, hastily spreading the news of it to those farther away, some of whom had settled down and lay at ease in their sublime majesty. Among them is Aphrodite, luxuriantly stretched out in Fig. 160 the right angle of the pediment, resting on the lap of her mother Dione. A seated figure is turned away from them – presumably the divine Leto, mother of Apollo and Artemis – toward the center, where her children probably stand. At the other side of the center Hera stands, sublime and dignified, directly next to Zeus. At a little distance, the youthfully blooming Hebe, Hera's daughter, hastens toward the left to the two Eleusinian goddesses, Demeter and Core, who are sitting on the chests of their secret cult. Near them in the left angle of the pediment Dionysos lies idly against a rock, corresponding to Aphrodite Fig. 159 on the right. His panther skin is spread over the rock, and he gazes out of the pediment, apparently in the direction where his sanctuary and theater lie, immediately adjacent to the

181

Fig. 161

161 *Western pediment of the*
     Parthenon. Acropolis, Athens.
     Drawing by Jacques Carrey.

hill of the Acropolis. In front of him, in the innermost corner of the pediment, Helios drives his team forth from the waves of the ocean, while to the right, matching him, Selene guides her team, with the famous primeval horse, into the depths, both as a sign that a great day has dawned for the gods.

The glorification of Athena Parthenos, the occupant of the temple, is also served by the group in the western pediment, where her strife with Poseidon for the Attic land is depicted. Thanks to the Carrey drawing, we can gain a complete idea of this group. The two pediments are differentiated here in the same way as they were in Olympia: the eastern pediment has more inner tension, with outward calm and restraint; the western has excitement, action, the discharge of tension. As Athena and Poseidon violently spring apart in the center, the motion surges on in turbulent waves, and breaks like surf in the angles of the pediment. The steeds of Athena's chariot rear up, and a female charioteer throws herself backward in order to rein them in. One of Kekrops' daughters leaps up in terror, the boy Erysichthon seeks refuge with the second, while the third presses closely against her father. Even the

162 *Leader of the sacrificial cattle.*
     Northern frieze of the Parthenon.
     Acropolis, Athens.
     Marble. 106 cm. high.

river god Kephissos, reclining in the extreme corner, is seized with violent motion. The figures in the right slope of the pediment are generally more calm in deportment, and are thoughtfully planned to correspond to those on the left. They are also attuned to one another in details. In the presence of this mature later work of Phidias, almost everything might be repeated that has already been said to characterize the statues of Polykletos, the other great sculptor of the classic period. Things that we usually consider opposites – experience and expression, object and invention, design and form, the spiritual and the sensual – here exist in complete harmony. And this unity of opposites is one of the supreme characteristics of the high classic period.

While, in Olympia, one god stands alone in the center of the pediment, in the western pediment of the Parthenon two divinities leave the actual center empty between them. This is apparently intended to express the idea that, at that time, the majestic presence of the gods alone was not enough for the center, that instead man must experience their power in violent action. No less significant is the fact that the land of Attica itself is drawn into the picture as the object of the gods' strife: the olive tree, the gift of Athena, which appears in the center of the pediment, can stand as its metaphor. In it is expressed the high-spirited self-esteem of the Athenians in the age of Pericles – the same feeling that is expressed at the end of Aeschylus' Oresteia (produced in the theater of Dionysos in 458), when Athena, on the same level as the Attic judges, places her vote in the urn. This familiarity between the gods and men of Greece had already been declared in the epics of Homer. There the gods intervened overwhelmingly in what was happening, in favor of their particular protégés. But now, in the classic period, Athena finds her place in the civic organization of the polis, and Attica is worth the strife of the gods. 'There truly the heavenly half of life was fitted to the semi-circular bowl of existence, as two full hemispheres merge into a complete golden globe' (Rilke).

In the Parthenon frieze, the city, the polis, takes the gods into her midst, as part of the balancing equation of life. At the great quadrennial festival of Panathenaea, the citizens of Athens honor their goddess Athena. The western frieze shows the procession preparing to start. The noble-born youths of Attica gird themselves and their horses for the journey, Fig. 162–166

163 *Hydria-bearers.*
     Northern frieze of the Parthenon.
     Acropolis, Athens.
     Marble. 106 cm. high.

164 Gods awaiting a festival procession. Eastern frieze of the Parthenon. Acropolis, Athens. Marble. 106 cm. high.

and mount their steeds. Exactly in the middle, intensifying the whole, there is a man seeking to hold in check his splendid, unruly horse – an authentic ancient Greek theme, man prevailing against the wildness and unruliness of nature. Immediately adjacent, two mounted youths hold back their impatient horses by force, bringing order to the insubordinate. Turning around the northwest corner to the northern side, the procession gets under way: an amazingly long cavalcade of riders, never handled unimaginatively, streaming broadly along, like an inexhaustible epic. Then come light chariots drawn by teams of four, each manned with a charioteer and an armed man. The procession seems to be straggling, and several chariots try to close up the gap at a flying gallop. As they reach the men walking ahead, several of the men turn to stop the running horses, so that the line of march will not be disrupted. The men probably make up the chorus which sings festive songs, accompanied by kitharists and players of aulos, a large number of whom proceed them. At the far

Fig. 163 east are bearers of gifts and leaders of the sacrificial rams and bulls. One of the hydria-bearers is in the act of lifting his hydria to his shoulder, an action that repeats for emphasis and clarity the theme of the whole frieze, a stopping, getting under way, and marching onward. The three youths in front of him, for all their similarity, are wonderfully differentiated in such details as the turning of the head, drapery, position of the hands, and expression. They

184

165 *Presentation of gifts for Athena. Eastern frieze of the Parthenon. Acropolis, Athens. Marble. 106 cm. high.*

have none of the mechanical uniformity of oriental art, but might serve instead as a metaphor of the typically Greek independence of the individual in the order of the whole. In Fig. 162 one of the groups of men leading bulls, the theme of controlling disruptive natural violence through human superiority is taken up again, with great plastic skill, in richly graduated relief. The reliefs are very flat, and every elevation retains its connection with the ground, so that there are no noticeable interruptions to the tangible solidity. But in this section there are so many plastic layers superimposed on one another that we wonder in amazement where the sculptor managed to obtain such convincing volume. As it continues on the eastern side, the procession arrives at its goal. Ahead of the steer-leaders are maidens with Fig. 166 precious utensils of sacrifice, with cups, jugs, and incense stands. Masters of ceremony walk among the maidens, who move in pairs at a solemn pace toward the center. The figures of five ancestral heroes make the transition to the gods who, enthroned in chairs, await the Fig. 164 procession. Here, for the third time on the Parthenon, unifying all the different picture cycles, appear the twelve highest Olympians, no longer fighting or performing great miracles, but taking part in the festival which the Athenians have prepared for them. In the exact center of the eastern frieze, surrounded by the gods, the priestess of the temple brings Fig. 165 chairs for the gods, and the high priest takes a peplos for Athena, acting out an extremely ancient custom. So real were their gods to the Greeks that they placed chairs for them to sit on and gave them clothes to dress in.

Pictorial art cannot, we assume, reproduce the passing of time; but the frieze of the Parthenon does exactly this in a unique fashion, since the one festive procession includes departure, progression, and arrival at the goal. The representation shares in the passing of time, from the west to the north, and from the south to the east; the passing time is always the present, in uninterrupted continuation, in the same way that the playing time coincides with the time of the action in a Greek drama. What later theorists have called the unity of time is here a oneness of time, actual time. This is the final touchstone for the solid, not merely imagined, reality of everything the Greeks created in their pictorial art. In addition to everything else, the representation of the festival procession of Panathenaea on the Parthenon is an historical picture, not an event that happened once, but the continuation into the living present of a piece of genuine, actual history. In the Parthenon frieze the Athenian people dedicate themselves to their goddess. Like the temple itself, the frieze is a votive offering, a work of piety. Through the centuries, the artistic power of the Greeks had grown into matchless perfection; yet at this, its highest peak, it was still not exalted as 'free art.' What the Greeks, in their masterpieces, gave to all ages as a memorial of their existence was the ceremonial shaping of life, the true realization of self.

166 *Procession of maidens and master of ceremonies. Eastern frieze of the Parthenon. Acropolis, Athens. Marble. 106 cm. high.*

Height of the amphora with cover, 67 cm. Berlin-Charlottenburg, Ehem. Staatliche Museen, Antikenabteilung.

92 Rhodian jug with animal frieze. Clay. 40 cm. high. Paris, Louvre.

93 Bowl by the Brygos Painter (detail). Clay. Diameter of the bowl, 32.5 cm. Paris, Louvre.

94 Brygos Painter: Priam begs Achilles to release Hector's body. Skyphos. Clay. 25 cm. high. Vienna, Kunsthistorisches Museum.

95 and 96 Skyphos by Pistoxenos (details). Clay. Height of the skyphos, 15 cm. Kunstgutlager Schloß Celle, formerly Schwerin, Mecklenburgisches Landesmuseum.

97 Orpheus among the Thracians. Crater (detail). Clay. Height of the crater, 51 cm. Berlin-Charlottenburg, Ehem. Staatliche Museen, Antikenabteilung.

98 Kleophon Painter: A warrior's farewell. Stamnos. Clay. 44 cm. high. Munich, Museum antiker Kleinkunst.

99 Erechtheum. Acropolis, Athens. Marble. – Cf. Fig. 121, 129, 130.

100 Attic jug. Clay. 21.5 cm. high. Berlin-Charlottenburg, Ehem. Stratliche Museen, Antikenabteilung.

101 Delphi. Sanctuary with Temple of Apollo.

102 Street of Lions in Delos. Marble.

103 Naxian sphinx in Delphi. Marble. 232 cm. high. Delphi, Museum.

104 Calf-bearer from the Acropolis. Marble. 165 cm. high. Athens, Acropolis Museum.

105 Nikandre from Delos. Marble. 175 cm. high. Athens, National Museum.

106 Small Cretan jug with plastic head of a woman. Clay. 10 cm. high. Berlin-Charlottenburg, Ehem. Staatliche Museen, Antikenabteilung.

107 'Woman of Auxerre' (detail). Poros. Height of the whole figure, 65 cm. Paris, Louvre.

108 and 109 Peplos Kore from the Acropolis. Marble. 118 cm. high. Athens, Acropolis Museum.

110 Kore from the Acropolis. Marble. 92 cm. high. Athens, Acropolis Museum.

111 Kore from the Acropolis. Marble. 54.3 cm. high. Athens, Acropolis Museum.

112 Female head from Olympia. Terra-cotta. 14 cm. high. Olympia, Museum.

113 Archaic polygonal masonry. Retaining wall of the Precinct of Athena, Delphi. Limestone.

114 Late archaic polygonal masonry. Retaining wall of the Temple of Apollo, Delphi. Limestone.

115 Archaic ashlar from the Letoon, Delos. Marble.

116 Retaining wall at the height of the Hellenistic period. Hellenistic Hall, Delos. Marble.

117 Treasury of the Athenians, Delphi. Marble.

118 and 119 Temple of Poseidon, Paestum. Limestone.

120 Tholos, Delphi. Marble.

121 Erechtheum. Acropolis, Athens. Marble. – Cf. Fig. 99, 129, 130.

122 Enneastylos, Paestum. Limestone.

123 Sketch of a Doric entablature.

124 Temple of Zeus, Olympia. Pediment end. Proportions. – Cf. Fig. 125, 144–153.

125 Temple of Zeus, Olympia. Ground plan. Reproduced from E. Curtius and F. Adler: *Olympia. Die Ergebnisse der vom Deutschen Reich veranstalteten Ausgrabungen*, Vol. II, Berlin, 1897, Plate 9. – Cf. Fig. 124, 144–153.

126 Parthenon. Acropolis, Athens. Ground plan. Reproduced from W. Hege and G. Rodenwaldt: *Die Akropolis*, Berlin, 1930. – Cf. Fig. 127, 157 to 166.

127 Parthenon. Acropolis, Athens. Marble. – Cf. Fig. 126, 157–166.

128 Temple of Athena Nike. Acropolis, Athens. Marble.

129 Erechtheum. Acropolis, Athens. Caryatid Portico. Marble. – Cf. Fig. 99, 121, 130.

130 Erechtheum. Acropolis, Athens. Ornament. Marble. – Cf. Fig. 99, 121, 129.

131 and 132 Temple of Artemis, Korkyra (Corfu). Pediment figures. Poros. Corfu, Museum. – Cf. Fig. 133.

133 Temple of Artemis, Korkyra (Corfu). Pediment end. Drawing. – Cf. Fig. 131, 132.

134 Old Temple of Athena. Acropolis, Athens. Pediments. Drawing. – Cf. Fig. 135, 136, 143.

135 and 136 Old Temple of Athena. Acropolis, Athens. Pediment figures. Poros. Athens, Acropolis Museum. – Cf. Fig. 134, 143.

137–139 Siphnian Treasury, Delphi. Eastern frieze. Marble. 64 cm. high. Delphi, Museum. – Cf. Fig. 140–142.

140 Siphnian Treasury, Delphi. Western frieze (detail). Marble. 64 cm. high. Delphi, Museum. – Cf. Fig. 137–139, 141, 142.

141 and 142 Siphnian Treasury, Delphi. Northern

frieze (details). Marble. 64 cm. high. Delphi, Museum. – Cf. Fig. 137–140.

143 Old Temple of Athena. Acropolis, Athens. Head of Athena from the eastern pediment. Marble. Height of the whole figure, c. 180 cm. Athens, Acropolis Museum. – Cf. Fig. 134–136.

144 Temple of Zeus, Olympia. Metope from the eastern end of the cella. Marble. 160 cm. high. Olympia, Museum. – Cf. Fig. 124, 125, 145–153.

145 Temple of Zeus, Olympia. Western end of the cella. Head of Athena from the Lion metope. Marble. Height of the metope, 160 cm. Olympia, Museum. – Cf. Fig. 124, 125, 144, 146–153.

146 Temple of Zeus, Olympia. Series of metopes on the western end of the cella. Drawing, reproduced from E. Curtius and F. Adler: *Olympia. Die Ergebnisse der vom Deutschen Reich veranstalteten Ausgrabungen.* Vol. III, Berlin, 1894, Pl. 45. – Cf. Fig. 124, 125, 144, 145, 147–153.

147 Temple of Zeus, Olympia. Series of metopes on the eastern end of the cella. Drawing, reproduced from E. Curtius and F. Adler: *Olympia. Die Ergebnisse der vom Deutschen Reich veranstalteten Ausgrabungen.* Vol. III, Berlin, 1894, Pl. 45. – Cf. Fig. 124, 125, 144–146, 148–153.

148 Temple of Zeus, Olympia. Central group from the eastern pediment. Marble. 330 cm. high. Olympia, Museum. – Cf. Fig. 124, 125, 144–147, 149–153.

149 Temple of Zeus, Olympia. Western end of the cella. Head of Athena from the Stymphalian metope. Marble. Height of the metope, 160 cm. Paris, Louvre. – Cf. Fig. 124, 125, 144–148, 150 to 153.

150 Temple of Zeus, Olympia. Eastern pediment. Boy. Marble. 105 cm. high. Olympia, Museum. – Cf. Fig. 124, 125, 144–149, 151–153.

151 Temple of Zeus, Olympia. Western pediment. Lapithan woman. Marble. 165 cm. high. Olympia, Museum. – Cf. Fig. 124, 125, 144–150, 152, 153.

152 Temple of Zeus, Olympia. Eastern end, right corner of pediment. Kladeos. Marble. 82.5 cm. high. Olympia, Museum. – Cf. Fig. 124, 125, 144–151, 153.

153 Temple of Zeus, Olympia. Western pediment. Head of a youth. Marble. Olympia, Museum. – Cf. Fig. 124, 125, 144–152.

154 Throne of Ludovisi. Side relief. Marble. 104 cm. high. Rome, Museo Nazionale delle Terme.

155 and 156 Dying child of Niobe. Marble. 149 cm. high. Rome, Museo Nazionale delle Terme.

157 and 158 Parthenon. Acropolis, Athens. Southern side. Centaur metopes. Marble. 134 cm. high. London, British Museum. – Cf. Fig. 126, 127, 159–166.

159 Parthenon. Acropolis, Athens. Eastern pediment. Dionysos. Marble. 121 cm. high. London, British Museum. – Cf. Fig. 126, 127, 157, 158, 160–166.

160 Parthenon. Acropolis, Athens. Eastern pediment. Aphrodite. Marble. 100 cm. high. London, British Museum. – Cf. Fig. 126, 127, 157–159, 161 to 166.

161 Parthenon. Acropolis, Athens. Western pediment. Drawing by Jacques Carrey. Paris, Bibliothèque Nationale. – Cf. Fig. 126, 127, 157–160, 162–166.

162 Parthenon. Acropolis, Athens. Northern frieze (detail). Marble. 106 cm. high. Athens, Acropolis Museum. – Cf. Fig. 126, 127, 157–161, 163–166.

163 Parthenon. Acropolis, Athens. Northern frieze (detail). Marble. 106 cm. high. Athens, Acropolis Museum. – Cf. Fig. 126, 127, 157–162, 164–166.

164 and 165 Parthenon. Acropolis, Athens. Eastern frieze (details). Marble. 106 cm. high. London, British Museum. – Cf. Fig. 126, 127, 157–163, 166.

166 Parthenon. Acropolis, Athens. Eastern frieze (detail). Marble. 106 cm. high. Paris, Louvre. – Cf. Fig. 126, 127, 157–165.

IDENTIFICATION OF THE VERBATIM QUOTATIONS

1. C. Picard, in: *Revue des études grecques*, Vol. 59/60, 1946/47, pp. 210ff.
2. B. Schweitzer: Der bildende Künstler und der Begriff des Künstlerischen in der Antike, in: *Neue Heidelberger Jahrbücher*, 1925, pp. 28ff., particularly pp. 77ff.
3. W. Jaeger: *Paideia. Die Formung des griechischen Menschen*, Vol. II, Berlin and Leipzig, 1944, p. 302.
4. Suidas *(Lexicon Graecum).* Under the word Θῆτες.
5. R. Harder: *Eigenart der Griechen.* Freiburg, 1949, p. 5ff.
6. W. Jaeger: *Paideia. Die Formung des griechischen Menschen*, Vol. I, Berlin and Leipzig, 1936, p. 175.
7. R. Harder: Die Meisterung der Schrift durch die Griechen, in: *Das neue Bild der Antike*, Vol. I, Leipzig, 1942, pp. 91ff., particularly p. 100.
8. W. Jaeger: *Paideia. Die Formung des griechischen Menschen.* Vol. I, Berlin and Leipzig, 1936, p. 175.
9. E. Buschor: *Griechische Vasen.* Munich, 1940, p. 15.
10. M. P. Nilsson: *Geschichte der griechischen Religion.* Vol. I, Munich, 1941, pp. 424ff., p. 442.
11. B. Snell: *Die Entdeckung des Geistes.* Hamburg, 1946, pp. 15ff., p. 22.
12. R. Harder: *Eigenart der Griechen.* Freiburg, 1949, p. 15.
13. W. Schadewaldt: *Legende von Homer, dem fahrenden Sänger.* Leipzig, 1942, p. 54f.
14. *Das Erwachen.* Songs and Fragments from the early age of Greece, translated, with introduction by Manfred Hausmann. Berlin, 1948, p. 31.
15. A. von Gerkan: Betrachtungen zum jonischen Gebälk, in: *Jahrbuch des Deutschen Archäologischen Instituts*, 61/62, 1946/47, p. 21.
16. W. Schadewaldt: *Sophokles und Athen.* Frankfurt a.M., 1935, p. 9.
17. E. Buschor: *Phidias der Mensch.* Munich, 1948, p. 45f. – E. Langlotz: *Phidiasprobleme.* Frankfurt a.M., 1947, p. 22ff.
18. W. Schadewaldt: *Sophokles und das Leid.* Potsdam, 1944, p. 20.

BLACK-AND-WHITE PHOTOGRAPHS

The photographer Friedrich Hewicker, Kaltenkirchen (Holstein), visited Greece and several of the great museums of Europe on assignment of the publisher. The following illustrations are reproduced here for the first time from his photographs: 1–3, 5, 6, 8, 9, 11, 17–20, 22, 23, 27–30, 39, 41–46, 51–54, 57, 59, 62, 65, 67, 76, 78, 85, 86, 88–90, 93, 95, 96, 101, 103, 105–110, 112, 114, 117, 121, 127–129, 137–142, 144, 145, 148–156, 166.

The other photographs are by Gustav Schwarz, Berlin: 12. – Ehem. Staatliche Museen, Berlin: 24, 97. – Fratelli Alinari, Florence: 25, 63, 64, 66, 71, 72. – Prof. W. Hege, Gelsenkirchen-Buer: 130–132. – British Museum, London: 164, 165. – F. L. Kennett, London (Courtesy LIFE MAGAZINE): 159, 160. – Bildarchiv Foto Marburg: 7, 13, 21, 26, 104, 111, 135, 136, 143, 162, 163. – Antikensammlungen, Munich: 34, 37, 38, 40. – Hirmer Verlag, Munich: 77, 80, 81, 83, 87, 98. – Franz Kaufmann, Munich: 4, 14, 15. – Verlag R. Piper & Co., Munich: 16. – Metropolitan Museum, New York: 56. – Archives Photographiques, Paris: 31. – Giraudon, Paris: 55, 73, 82, 84, 161. – Kunsthistorisches Museum, Vienna: 94.

COLOR PHOTOGRAPHS

Ralph Kleinhempel, Hamburg: 61, 69, 70, 74, 75, 91, 100. – Friedrich Hewicker, Kaltenkirchen (Holstein): 60, 68, 92, 99.